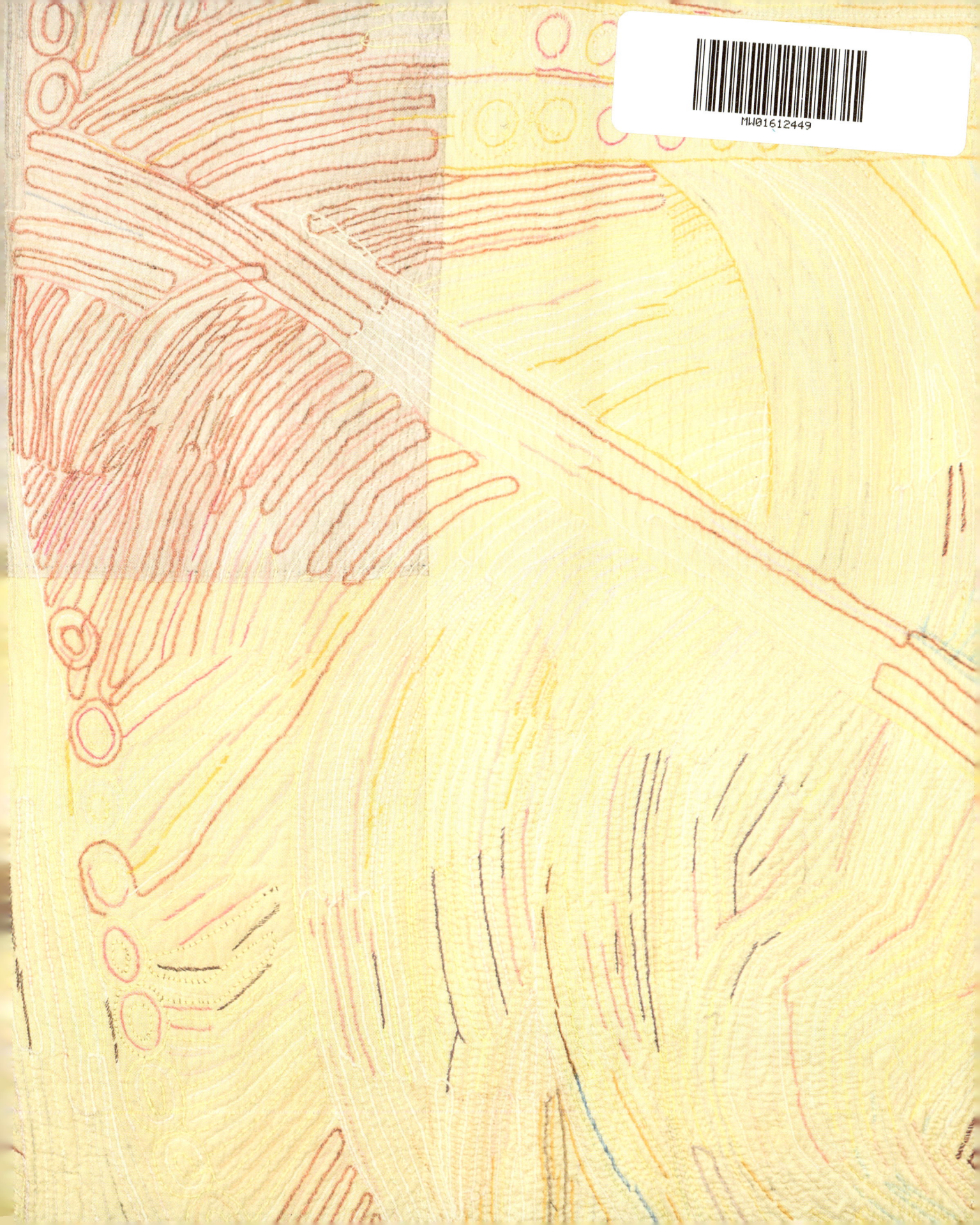

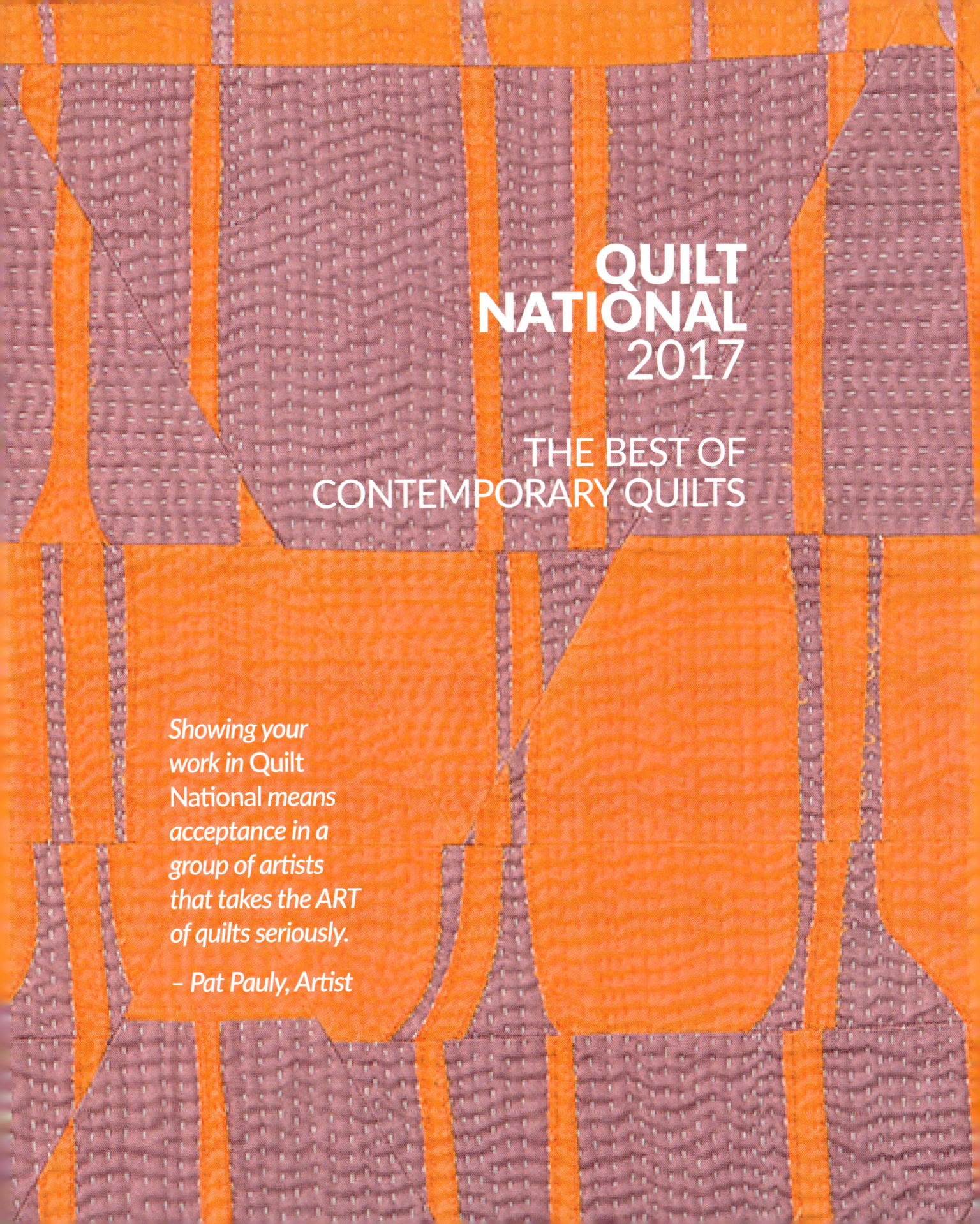

QUILT
NATIONAL
2017

THE BEST OF
CONTEMPORARY QUILTS

Showing your work in Quilt National *means acceptance in a group of artists that takes the ART of quilts seriously.*

– Pat Pauly, Artist

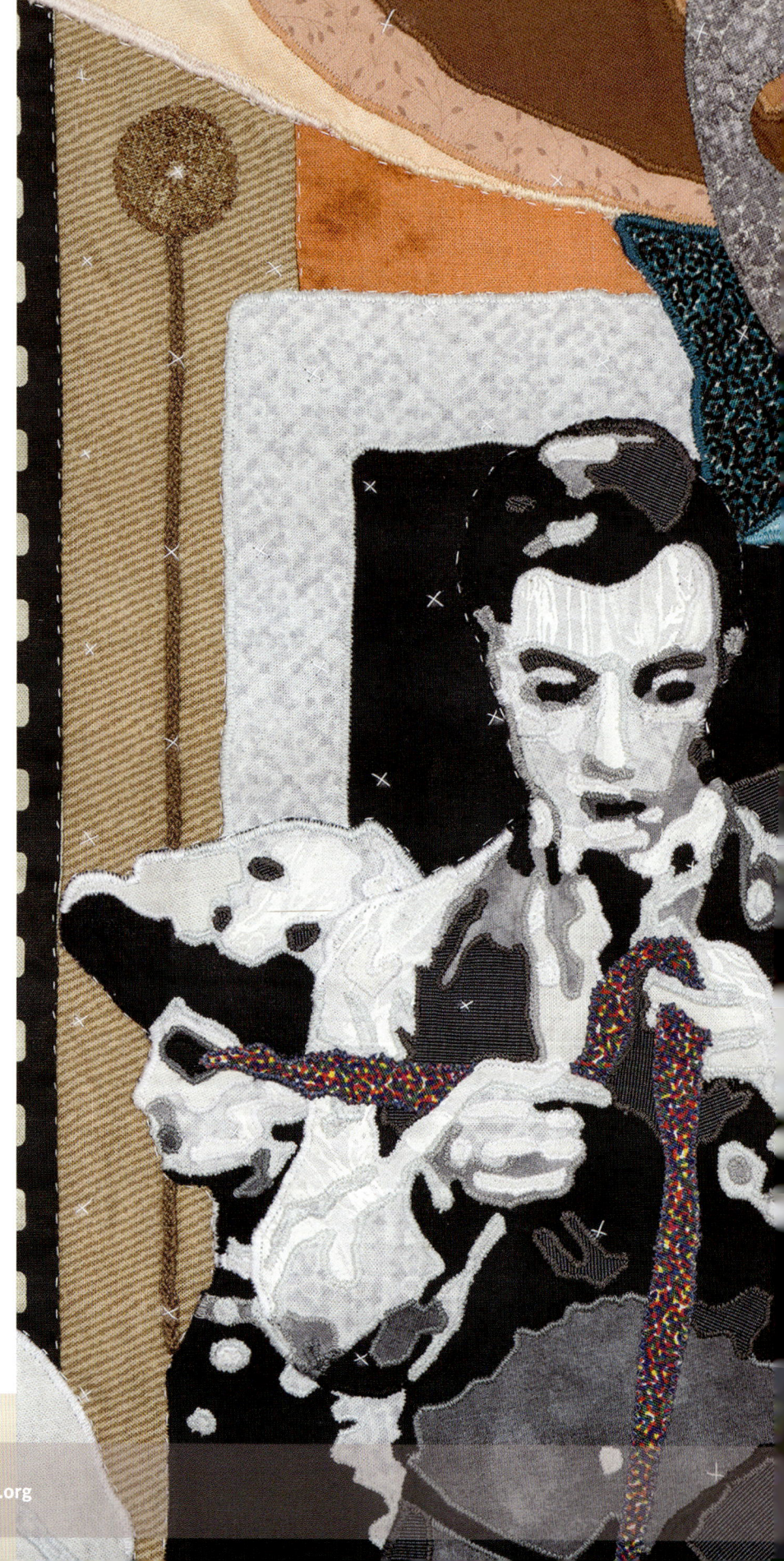

Dairy Barn Arts Center
Executive Director: **Jane Forrest Redfern**
Exhibition Manager: **Kelsey Dillow**
Editor: **Anita C. James**
Photographers: **Sam Girton, Gary J. Kirksey,
Lawrence Hamel-Lambert**
Cover Quilt: **Prometheus** by Kerri Green
Endpaper Quilt: **Soft Summer Gone** by Judith E. Martin

Our *Quilt National '17* Sponsors:

Friends of Fiber Arts

Nihon Vogue Co., Ltd/
Japan Handicrafts Instructors' Association

Friends of Fiber Art International

Athens County Convention and Visitors Bureau

eQuilter.com

Ohio University Inn and Conference Center

The Crow Barn Art Retreats, Baltimore, Ohio,
www.nancycrow.com

Hampton Inn

Nelsonville Quilt Company

Ohio Quilts

Ohio Arts Council

National Endowment for the Arts

Porter Financial Services

Quilt Surface Design Symposium

Studio Art Quilt Associates

With additional support
from the following individuals:

Marvin Fletcher

Corrine Brown

David Hendricker

Many thanks to long-time supporter:

The Ardis and Robert James Foundation

Library of Congress Control Number 2017935128
Quilt National 2017: The Best of Contemporary Quilts
Published by The Dairy Barn Arts Center, Athens, Ohio
www.dairybarn.org

ISBN 978-0-692-81328-7

Design, editorial,
& production services
Fiber Art
now

A division of
**M. Young &
Associates, Inc.**

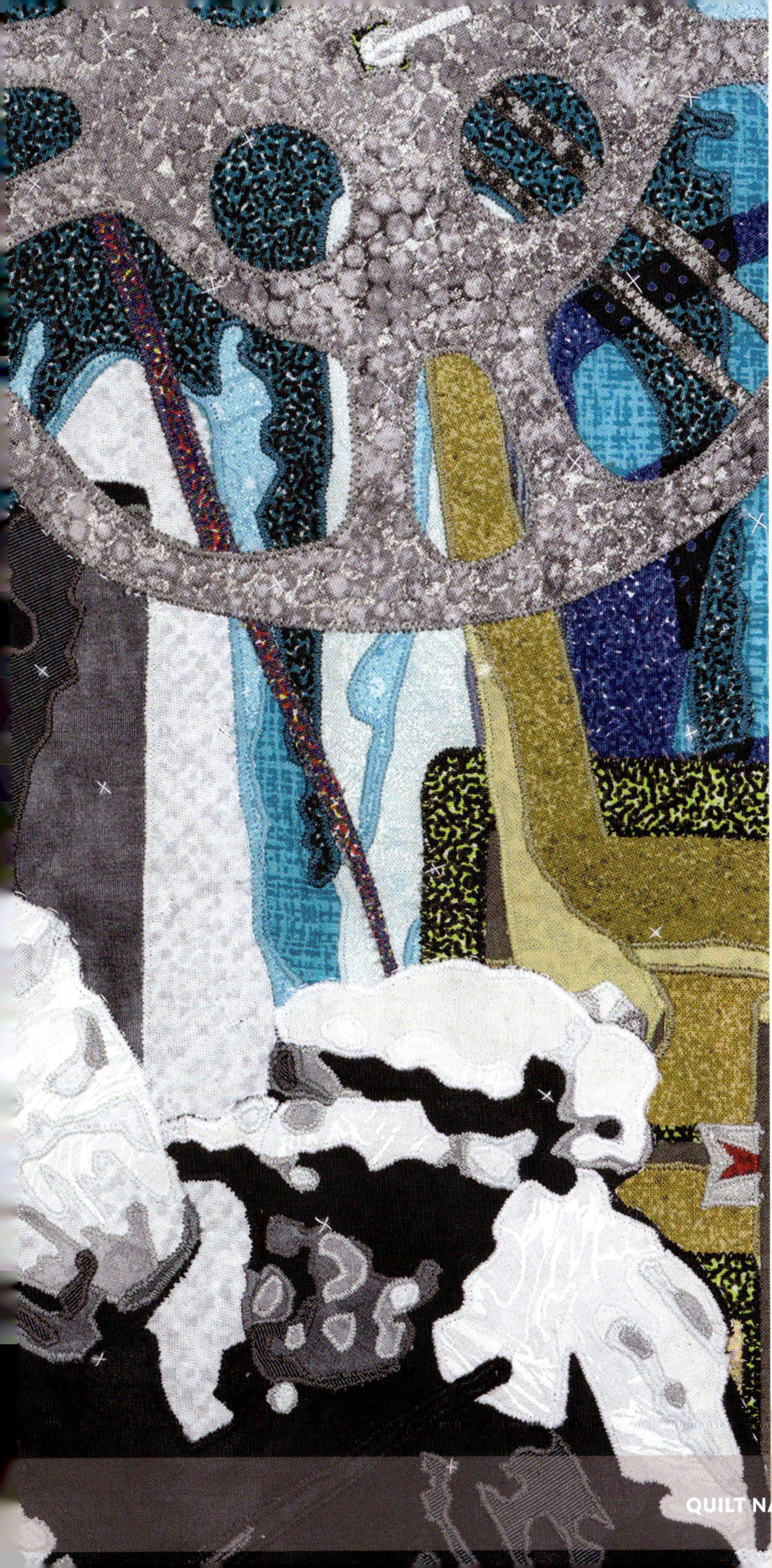

Dedicated to Karen Nulf, former Quilt National catalog graphic designer, board member, and friend.

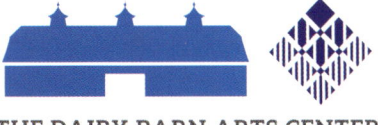

THE DAIRY BARN ARTS CENTER

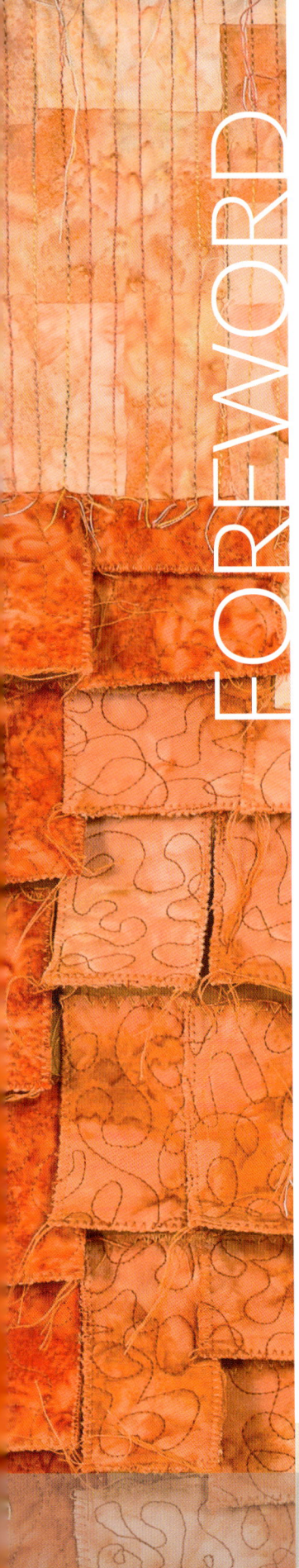

I n 2017, as we reach the 20th biennial of *Quilt National*, we celebrate the artists from all over the world who have participated. Since 1979 when we presented our first *Quilt National*, 9,946 artists have submitted 20,463 quilts for consideration. We have had 1,552 quilts by 798 artists on exhibition selected by 20 panels of jurors. The artists have been from as close as two miles away to across the United States and throughout the world. Twenty *Quilt Nationals* later, artists from around the world continue to share their work with us, in order to bring the best in contemporary quilts to the public.

It is not only the accepted artists who have been the lifeblood of *Quilt National*, but also all of the artists who have submitted their works. We celebrate the accepted artists, and also those who have submitted, not just one time, but five or six times. Hilary Fletcher found this to be an incredible testament to the outstanding longevity and prestige of *Quilt National*—that artists would try repeatedly to be juried into the exhibition. To honor that spirit, she founded the "Persistent Pays Award" which we will give to two artists this year who have tried five times. It is this level of commitment from artists that encourages us to continue the history and legacy that *Quilt National* brings to our organization and to the world of contemporary art.

Our 20th biennial celebration began by asking Nancy Crow to be one of the jurors. We also invited Petra Fallaux, a writer, curator, creative director, and artist, and Art Martin, the associate curator/collections manager at the Muskegon Museum of Art. These individuals outline their experience as jurors in the pages to come and we hope you enjoy reading their reflections on the works accepted into the exhibition.

We could not have sustained *Quilt National* without the commitment of our community, members, sponsors, and individuals, as well as organizations sponsoring awards, and individuals helping with the jurying process, the maintenance of the databases, and the overall process. We have been blessed to have had incredible directors of *Quilt National*, especially Hilary Fletcher and Kathleen Dawson, and now to have as exhibitions manager, Kelsey Dillow. Their passion has been exceptional and has ensured that everything was correct and organized, and that the quilts were handled with care here and abroad.

Quilt National has toured to Canada, France, and Japan, in addition to 86 museums and sites in 32 states across the United States, thus exposing thousands of people to contemporary quilts. This summer Athens, Ohio, is celebrating with us so, please, come and check out our Quilt Crawl along the streets of our city and region to see a wide variety of quilts that celebrate the art form. We invite you to visit our newly expanded arts center and to share with us some of the stories, experiences, and history of how *Quilt National* has changed you!

Jane Forrest Redfern
Executive Director, Dairy Barn Arts Center

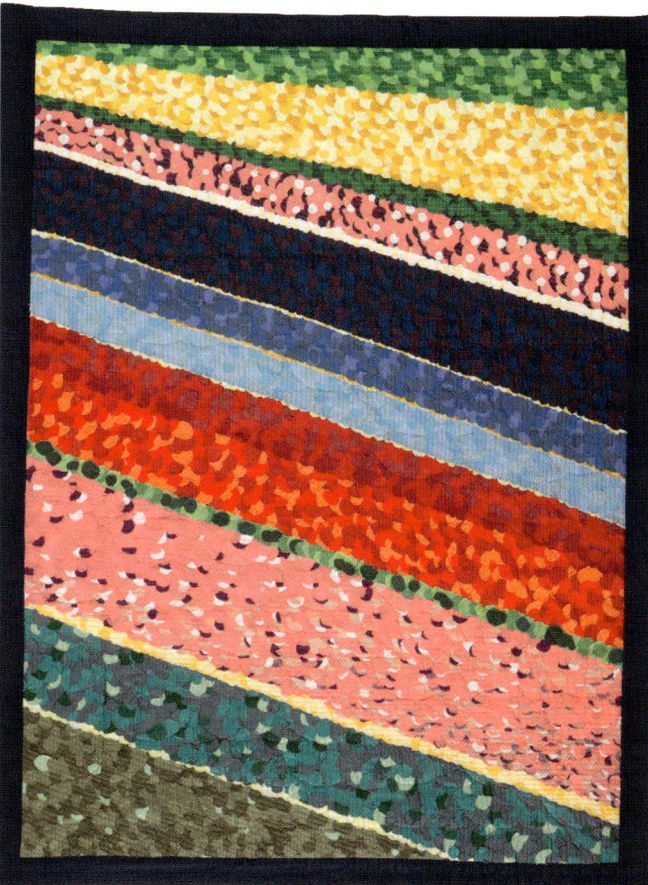

Holley Junker, **Flowerseed Farm**

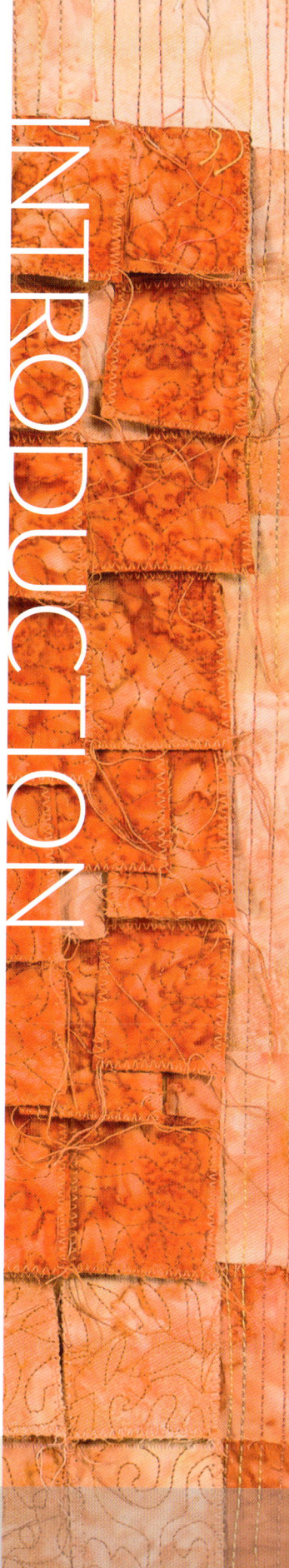

I am very excited to share *Quilt National '17* with the readers of this book and the visitors to the Dairy Barn. My late wife, Hilary, and I were involved with this show from the first exhibition in 1979 and have watched it grow and fulfill the dreams of its three founders. For more than 25 years Hilary worked with *Quilt National* as a volunteer and then as project director. I have also volunteered in a variety of roles.

Quilt National was also the venue that started our collection of studio art quilts. In May 1985, as our 20th wedding anniversary approached, and *Quilt National '85* was getting ready for its debut, some of the Dairy Barn staff suggested that I buy Hilary one of the quilts in the show as an anniversary present. The staff told me that she particularly admired Holley Junker's *Flowerseed Farm*. I bought the quilt, but did not tell Hilary about the purchase. Early on the morning of June 8, our wedding anniversary, I woke Hilary and told her that I had purchased Holley's quilt as an anniversary present. She was overjoyed.

Hilary had told others that, once they bought a quilt for display, they needed to limit its exposure to light and should do that by collecting even more quilts to hang. We began to follow this piece of advice. Over the years, we added others to Holley's quilt; often buying quilts submitted to *Quilt National*.

Quilt National continues to be an introduction to the wonderful world of studio art quilts. I enjoy and admire the creativity and artistic expression of the many amazingly talented artists throughout the world.

Marvin Fletcher

MARVIN FLETCHER is a retired history professor, quilt collector, and volunteer at the Dairy Barn for many events, including many Quilt Nationals, both during the jury process and at the exhibition itself.

Quilt National *introduced me to many fine quilt artists and collectors who are still important to my four decades as an artist. I have found doors opening because of being in* Quilt National. *Being a juror in 1997 gave me an opportunity to be on the other side of the curtain and to give back to the medium that has given me such sustaining pleasure.*

– Joan Schulze, Artist

CELEBRATING
QUILT NATIONAL

FROM THE
BEGINNING...

When early settlers arrived in America they brought with them much of their cultural heritage from Europe—including the art of quilting. Though this domestic craft lost its lure and luster in the period following World War II, a movement took hold in the late 1970s that transformed the art of the quilt into a hip and innovative art form. This vibrant rebirth in quilt making had its roots in rebellion and was influenced by America's Bicentennial, the feminist movement, and the desire by fine artists to integrate modern treatments into traditional arts and crafts. The history of this movement, which has been documented and published by a host of art historians, is never told without mention of the catalyst that united and challenged these contemporary artists—*Quilt National*.

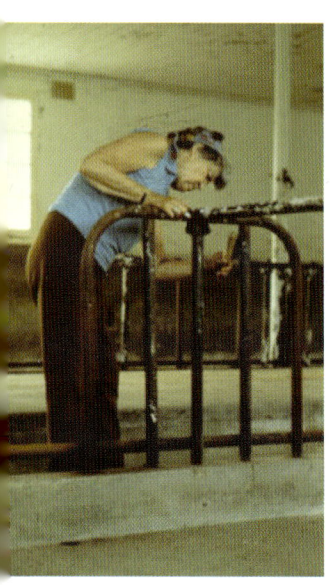

Some of the key motivators of the art quilt movement lived in Athens, Ohio, in the late 1970s. Nancy Crow, Françoise Barnes, Virginia Randles, and other artists in the Buckeye State were creating contemporary compositions with strong colors and bold designs that were considered unacceptable to the organizers of traditional quilt shows. The only exhibit opportunities for these artists were in mixed media fiber shows—alongside baskets, rugs, and other weavings. Driven by the desire to showcase what are now known as "contemporary quilts," Crow devised a plan. She, Barnes, and a host of other dedicated volunteers distributed entry forms, developed a jury process, and organized an exhibit devoted entirely to this new breed of art.

Their search for an exhibit venue serendipitously coincided with the efforts of Harriet and Ora Anderson, area artists, and civic-minded citizens to preserve an abandoned dairy barn sitting quietly on the crest of a gently sloping hill. Situated on grounds belonging to Athens State Hospital, the barn was scheduled to be razed in 1978, but a citizen's task force committee and the Hocking Valley Arts Council succeeded in their petition to preserve the structure. In 1978 the building was placed on the National Register of Historic Places and The Dairy Barn Southeastern Ohio Cultural Arts Center was born.

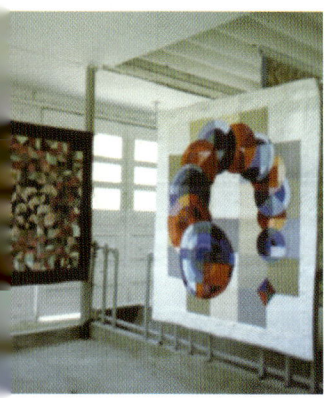

Quilt National '79 was the first major exhibition at the newly organized Dairy Barn Arts Center. There were 390 works submitted for this premier exhibit from 196 artists. The response of viewers varied—some were perplexed by the unexpected compositions while others were enthralled. "Phenomenal! Splendid!" said Françoise Barnes on seeing the vertically hung, large-scale expressive works of art that were clearly not bedcoverings. Barnes realized that she was looking at history in the making. "It was obvious that we were groundbreakers—taking off on a road that had not been traveled before. I knew then that great things were going to follow."

Barnes' instincts were spot on. *Quilt National's* renown continued to gain momentum over the years, due largely to the efforts of Athens resident Hilary Morrow Fletcher. Fletcher, like Barnes, was captivated by the visual impact of the exhibition—she experienced an "epiphany" when she walked through the doors in 1979. "This is the first *Quilt National* of the 21st century," she is noted to have said. "As we travel the path to the future it seems like a good time to consider where we have been, where we are now, and where this path might take us in the years to come."

Armed with this vision, Hilary Fletcher became the Quilt National Project Director in March 1982, where she served until her death in 2006. Through her diligence, she succeeded in building a foundation for an exhibit that began as one that reached across the nation into one that spanned the globe. She traveled extensively, speaking about the history and evolution of the art quilt. "Hilary opened my eyes to the world of studio quilters," said Judy Schwender, curator of collections at The National Quilt Museum in Paducah, Kentucky. "She taught me the difference between 'classic' quilts and 'innovative' quilts. She preferred those terms to 'traditional' and 'art' quilts."

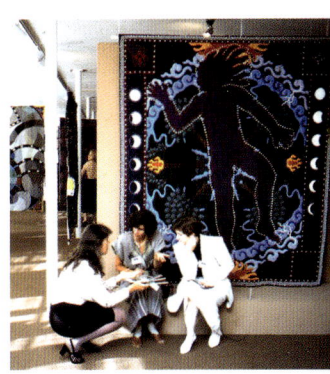

Quilt National has been the most important ongoing forum for the innovative quilt since its inception. "Without *Quilt National*, I believe that a great deal of the creativity seen at national and international shows would not be as vibrant," said Schwender. "They were the pioneers that set the bar for contemporary quilts," said Gul Laporte, international exhibitions coordinator for Studio Art Quilters Association. "It had a very prestigious reputation in Europe, and French artists were excited about submitting their quilts."

Quilt National continues to be the premier venue for the work of many major artists whose names have become synonymous with the genre. One such artist, Katie Pasquini Masopust, has been juried into *Quilt National* four times—winning the Quilts Japan Prize, and serving as a juror in 2009. "When I began quilt making in 1978, it was my fantasy to be included in *Quilt National*. Every year that I get in validates my work," said Masopust. "This is like the Academy Awards of quilt making. It reflects the work of the top art quilters in the world and what they are doing at the present time."

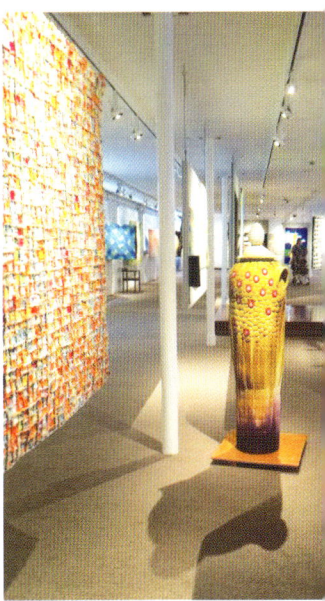

Thanks to *Quilt National*, these works of art have entered the permanent collections of major public arts institutions and organizations around the world that are exclusively devoted to the collection, exhibition, and documentation of textiles. Five-time exhibitor Pam RuBert saw her first traveling *Quilt National* exhibit at The City Museum in Saint Louis, Missouri, in 2003. She bought the catalog and immersed herself in the exhibit for hours. Though inspired by the abstract designs, the freedom of spirit of *Quilt National* moved her to return to and embrace her creative roots. She had been crafting her unique cartoon-style quilts for only a year when her work was accepted into *Quilt National '05*. "Being part of *Quilt National* and associated with other accepted artists was huge for my career," said RuBert. "*Quilt National* has exposed me to a broader audience...the show has a great history, is well run, and caters to collectors. The exhibit catalogs are well done and well distributed."

Nearly 8,000 visitors flock to this historic college town every other year—the only place to see *Quilt National* in its entirety. Following its Dairy Barn debut, the collection is broken down into traveling exhibits and circulates for approximately two years, gracing museums and art institutions from coast to coast and across the globe. Nearly four decades and 20 exhibitions later, its purpose remains the same: to carry the definition of quilting far beyond its traditional parameters and to promote quilt making as what it always has been—an art form.

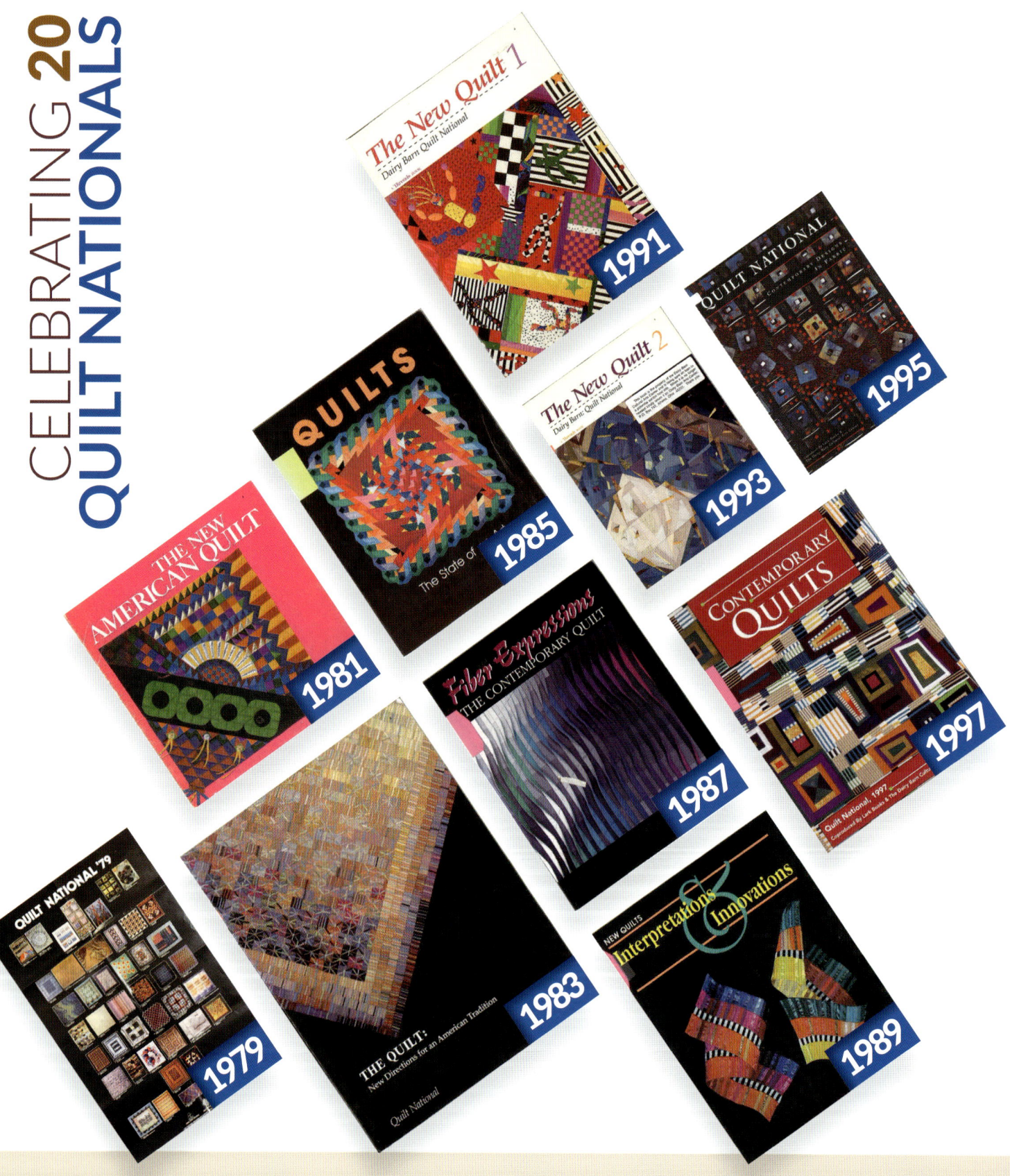

1979	Michael James Gary Schwindler Renee Seidel	1989	Chris Wolf Edmonds Bernard Kester Yvonne Porcella	1997	Nancy Halpern Jason Pollen Joan Schulze	2009	Sue Benner Katie Pasquini Masopust Ned Wert
1981	H. Daniel Butts III Nancy Crow Diane Itter	1991	Tafi Brown Esther Parkhurst Rebecca A. T. Stevens	1999	Nancy Crow Caryl Bryer Fallert-Gentry Bruce Pepich	2011	Eleanor McCain Pauline Verbeek-Cowart Nelda Warkentin
1983	Nancy Crow Michael James Joy Nixon	1993	Judi Warren Blaydon Elizabeth Busch Michael Monroe	2001	Melissa Leventon Arturo Alonzo Sandoval Jane A. Sassaman	2013	Linda Colsh Judith Content Penny McMorris
1985	Lloyd Herman David Hornung Terrie Hancock Mangat	1995	Ann Batchelder Libby Lehman Linda R. MacDonald	2003	Liz Axford Wendy Huhn Robert Shaw	2015	Rosalie Dace Ann Johnston Judy Schwender
1987	Gerhardt Knodel Penny McMorris Jan Myers-Newbury			2005	Mark Richard Leach M. Joan Lintault Miriam Nathan-Roberts	2017	Nancy Crow Petra Fallaux Art Martin
				2007	Tim Harding Paula Nadelstern Robin Treen		

1999

2005

2011

2015

2001

2007

2013

2009

2003

USE & REUSE:
THE VALUE OF PRESERVATION

Many of today's artists make use of recycled materials such as bottle caps, paper, and fabric. The terms upcycle, recycle, reimagine, repurpose, and adaptive reuse pepper the statements of artists and curators alike. Many of these words are new to our language, but the concepts of reusing material, of eliminating waste, and of preserving our past are deeply embedded in our culture—quilt making, which sprang from the desire to make use of fragments of fabric, embodies these ideals.

What more fitting a site for *Quilt National*, the premiere global exhibition of contemporary quilt art, than the Dairy Barn Art Center of Athens, Ohio, a building of Georgian Revival architectural influence that had fallen into disuse and was saved from demolition by a group of artists? The artists, led by Harriet and Ora Anderson, reimagined and created a future by preserving a piece of the past.

It has been said that, at its best, preservation engages the past in a conversation with the present over a mutual concern for the future.
-William Murtagh, first keeper of the National Register of Historic Places

Built in 1914 by The Athens Asylum for the Insane (later called the Athens State Hospital), the building served as a dairy barn, which furnished milk and dairy products for the institution and also provided therapeutic work and job training for patients, until the mid-1960s when the dairy was finally closed.

As Ora Anderson told the tale, one day in 1977, he and his wife, Harriet, an art teacher and professional artist, were enjoying fresh-caught fish and cocktails on their deck with five of their friends. They were lamenting the lack of places to display art in the Athens area, when Harriett said that there was an old, unused dairy barn out at the mental health center that might be available. It had been abandoned for ten years.

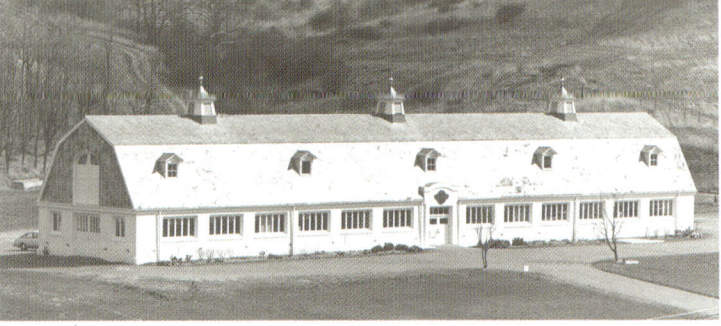

The seven of them drove out to the barn right then to have a look, and found a crew already demolishing one of the outbuildings. The contractor told them that he had a contract to tear it all down. Faced with that inevitability, Harriet dug in her heels and said, "No, this is not going to happen!"[1]

Harriet promptly crafted a letter to the Ohio Director of Properties for the Mental Health Centers of Ohio outlining a plan to turn the building into an arts center, to preserve an "architectural gem" and to "foster and preserve the skills, folk arts, and talents so abundant in Southeastern Ohio." She asked for time, "time to explore the possibilities, time to explore and plan curriculum, time to study financing, and time to determine the total extent of interest throughout the area."[2]

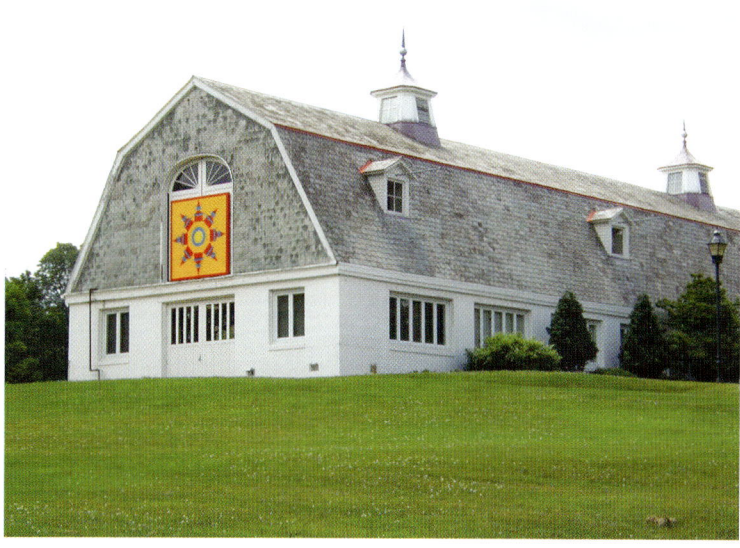

The following Monday, on Harriet's instructions, Ora, a former state lobbyist, went to Columbus to talk to his friend Governor Jim Rhodes about the barn. At the end of that meeting, the governor picked up the phone, called the director of the mental health department for the state, and told him that Ora wanted the old dairy barn, and he was to make sure Ora got it.

And so began the journey from dairy barn to art center.

The group of artists were given a $5.00-a-year lease for three years, during which time they were to establish an art center that was recognized by the greater art community in the state. If they succeeded, the barn would be given to the organization they established.

The artists set about cleaning up this long-abandoned cow barn—which was no small feat. The milking area, including the gutters that held cow manure, had not been cleaned out for ten years; the troughs that had held feed, and the stanchions that secured the cows while they were being milked were still in place; the hayloft, full of "record setting cobwebs" and mounds of old, dusty, and broken-down hay, had gaps between the floorboards so that hay hung down through the cracks into the large area below. The roof needed repair.

The intrepid band of artists, which quickly grew to 10, and then 15, chipped out the manure troughs with pick and shovel. They wrote grants and enlisted volunteers to repair the enormous roof, to physically remove the stanchions, and to fill and seal the newly-emptied manure gutters and feed troughs with concrete. They also formed a nonprofit corporation, applied for grants, and began creating programming.

In 1978 The Athens State Hospital Cow Barn was placed on the National Register of Historic Places as being of value for its architectural, agricultural, and social history, and in 1979 they mounted their first full-scale art exhibition, *Quilt National '79*, thereby transforming an ending into a beginning.   *— DairyBarn.org*

1 "Ora Anderson on Harriet and the Dairy Barn," *www.youtube.com/watch ?v=PbTTxTuoHEc&list= PLDA69A7F4495AFBF*

2 "Letter to AMH from Harriet Anderson," *http://dairybarn.org*

THE JURORS

For me, the most important aspect of a Quilt National acceptance is becoming part of the history of displaying the quilt as an art form. My name was placed alongside those who were pioneers in the medium, those who were represented in Quilt National exhibits at the very beginning. What a thrill!

– Pat Budge, Artist

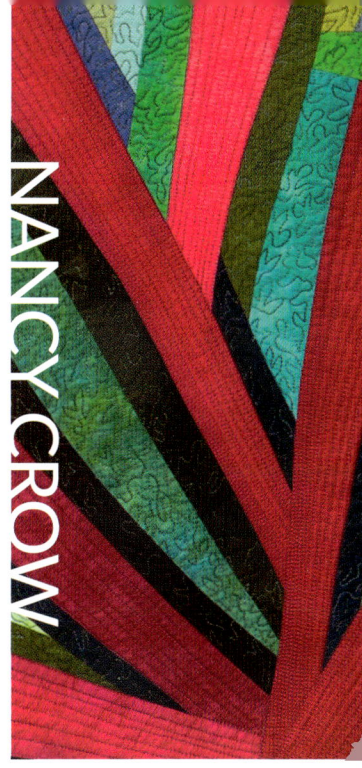

Wow! What a rich variety of works greet viewers of *Quilt National '17*. As a juror, I was thrilled to see so many strong quilts entered by artists whose work I did not know and additionally thrilled by the astounding new growth shown by seasoned artists known for their singular earlier styles. It is wonderful to witness this commitment to exploration and change! Diversity? Yes—an abundance of diversity in visual information punctuates this dynamic and cohesive exhibition. In all categories, I found that the best works exhibited dramatically strong ideas combined with dedicated techniques that were skillfully executed. Throughout the two days, we three jurors worked easily together, assigning numbers to each entry, and then waiting till the very end of this process to talk about what had been chosen. At that time we discovered that all of us had come to nearly the same conclusions, making it easy to finalize the selection of works.

In writing my essay for this catalog, I decided I wanted to address a variety of important issues regarding quilts that were entered but which were not accepted. These were recurrent issues I noted in the vast array of entries we reviewed. It has been years since I last juried a *Quilt National* competition, and soon it will be 40 years since the very first *Quilt National* opened in 1979. I arrived in Athens with mixed feelings of trepidation knowing how strongly I feel that quilts must be held to the same high standards as any other art form, created with excellence in mind, and honored. I expected and hoped to see a depth of exploration of ideas emphasizing and supporting a strong individual voice. I acknowledged to myself that any participating artist must convince me of his or her seriousness as a quilt maker. Otherwise, why enter a quilt competition? I also hoped that I would see many, many large works because I feel strongly that quilt exhibitions today too often emphasize only-small-to-medium-size quilts. However, the truths found in the huge number of entries were quite mixed and I felt perplexed by the end of the first jury day.

As we viewed the images—images that were not arranged in any particular order as to subject matter, style, technique, size, etc.—I was struck that so many quilt makers exhibited no individual voice. To have an individual voice, I believe one must first have an idea to which one is committed to exploring in-depth till the soul shines through. Next, I believe the artist must employ technique(s) so fluently as to convincingly bring the idea into being. Next, I believe one must work with a deeply personal color vocabulary, whether vast or very simple, but which clearly supports and emphasizes the idea. Finally, I believe one must employ a format (usually at the very beginning of the process) to organize all the information into a final cohesive composition. For any prolific artist, the same strong format can be used over and over as in a long series helping to establish the artist's individual voice. Think Agnes Martin! Richard Diebenkorn! Mondrian! Martin Ramirez! Mark Bradford! Chuck Close! Lee Krasner! Anna Williams! The point of my emphasizing all of this is that after viewing dozens and dozens of works that seemed unattached to anyone or anything, but strangely so alike from one to the next, and yet, with nothing distinguishing one from the other, I realized this was most often due—importantly—to the lack of any insistent voice, idea, format. An enormous assortment of surface design techniques thrown at squares and rectangles and then combined into an uninspired composition is uninspired. Most often, among the entries we viewed, there was a filling up of the picture plane with surface design or geometric shapes or stitching, but there was no sense of spatial tension or even a "why" it was all thrown together. This

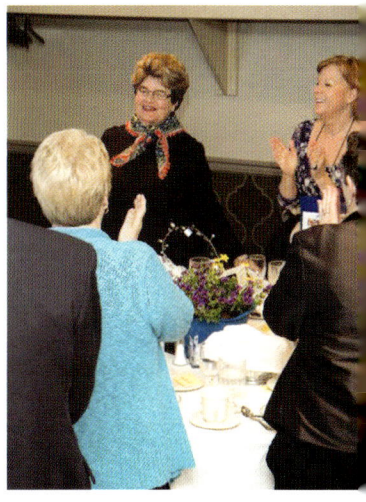

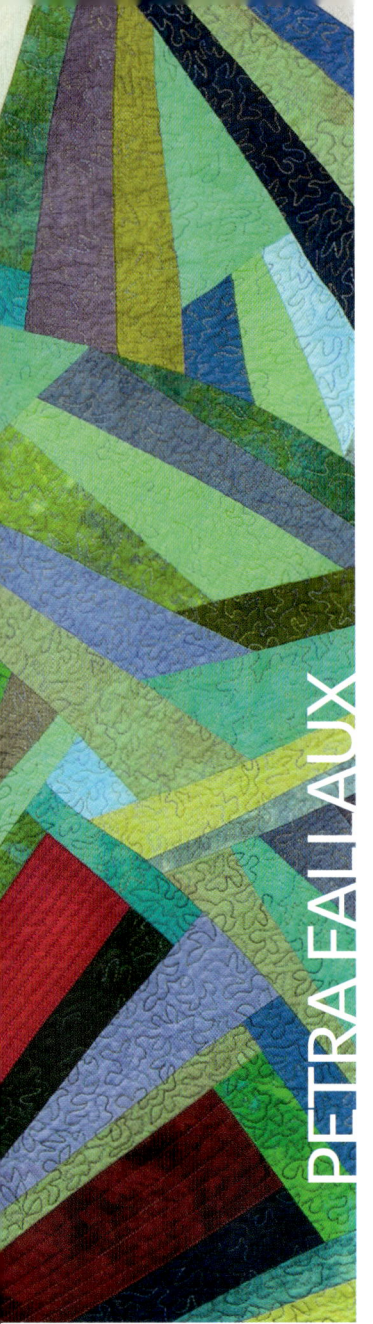

PETRA FALLAUX

left the nagging question: "How about just getting down to the hard work of making great quilts, many, many, many of them, one after the other—till the individual voice gets strongly established—before even entering major competitions?"

Overall, the works juried into *Quilt National '17* were created by artists in charge of their ideas. This is reflected in the evidence that many dug deeper, spending hours doing the slogging to find out who they really are, finding where their fresh ideas reside, ideas connected to them and their experiences. This is so important—to be rigorous in finding one's individual strengths. These artists understand why they are making quilts.

We are at a turning point in contemporary quilt making and I believe *Quilt National's* mission is to establish and seek excellence as it celebrates quilts as an art form. Many of the included artists clearly have given heart and soul to create some of the best work of their careers and I emphatically congratulate them!

Art is personal. The engine that drives you to make it must roar from within you. Art selected for a juried show like *Quilt National* is judged relative to the other work submitted. Add to this the personal proclivities of the jurors, and you have several reasons to take the result as one version of many possible exhibitions. As such, a fortuitous spot in a juried show can't be the driving motivation behind making your work, nor should a serendipitous absence stop you in your tracks.

Many people will have personal opinions of your work. Jurying *Quilt National* is both professional and personal. My professional eye has been trained during years of organizing contemporary art exhibitions. Works that first attract my attention ooze tension, intention, and invention. If I know the work to have come from a sustained path of inquiry, I look for risks taken to break new ground. I want to see work that illuminates rich inspiration and serious aspirations.

Poring over the entries as a fellow artist, I have immediate responses of appreciation ranging from "I wish I had made that." to "I could never do that." I admire complex compositions with intricate qualities that I would love to emulate but know I will never pursue because I am not cut out of the same cloth. I marvel at works with flawless applications of screen and mono printing on cloth, surface design techniques that I am trying to perfect myself. I am the first to admit that I quickly surrender to humor and not at all easily to the overtly political. My affinity is with abstraction: contemplative, introspective, or meditative works that bring me quiet moments of awe rather than wow.

Making any kind of quilt is a notoriously time-consuming undertaking. Many quilts in this exhibit are testimony to dogged pursuits. Among the entries, I sensed less out-of-the-box thinking and more honing and perfecting. Artists are actively deepening rather than broadening their work. Mark making with dye applications, hand stitching, and machine quilting have especially evolved through increased proficiency rather than forced innovation. Surface design can attain a soft, painterly elegance while refined layering creates densely colorful compositions. Stark repetition of graphic elements is found through dye applications as well as through piecing.

My fellow jurors added both historical depth of knowledge and a fresh eye: Artist Nancy Crow bravely chose quilts as her medium, stood famously at the bedrock of *Quilt National*, and has never let up pursuing her art, while Art Martin recently became an earnest and enthusiastic champion fully committed to organizing quilt exhibitions at his museum. It was with considerable ease that we selected over half of the show and we readily agreed on the awards. Discussions to round out and complete the exhibition were hard, as each one of us saw the elimination of personal favorites. In the end, to our pleasant surprise, a third of our selections were first-time entrants, securing new voices and welcome additions to the canon of *Quilt National* artists.

The driving motor behind the first *Quilt National* at the Dairy Barn in 1979 was "to provide an exhibit opportunity to artists whose work was unwelcome by the organizers of the existing quilt shows." This original impetus has resulted in a rich, tangible, and continuous biennial history of thought-provoking *Quilt Nationals*. Today, *Quilt National* is an art exhibition among many others of its kind, but it will forever be the first of its kind. To have been asked to jury and assemble *Quilt National '17* is a great honor. It is my hope that this twentieth rendition is another inspiring survey of contemporary artists who make both proficient and personal work worth contemplating, and yes, worth celebrating.

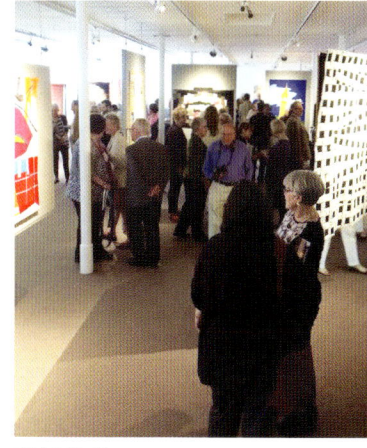

2015 Quilt National opening

It was a privilege to serve as one of the jurors for the 20th biennial of *Quilt National*. Jane Forest Redfern, executive director of the Dairy Barn, and her staff and volunteers worked diligently to guide us through the process of evaluating 748 entries. Their love of the show was apparent, and the legacy of this groundbreaking exhibition is clearly in wonderful hands. My thanks to fellow jurors Nancy Crow and Petra Fallaux, whose passion for art, and specifically for contemporary quilts, made this experience a truly memorable one.

In jurying a body of entries, comparisons are necessarily made and judgments are based not only on the inherent qualities of an artwork, but on how those qualities compare to other entries in the show. Strength of design, technical skill, color, conceptual content, creativity, and innovation are all weighed. Equally important, however, from the perspective of the juror, is to gather a body of work that effectively conveys a story and informs and inspires artists and art admirers alike. While personal taste is an unavoidable factor, as a juror I believe it is critical that the final selection of art reflects the nature of the entries. A strong show should capture, as much as possible, a sense of the now, of what contemporary artists are engaged with, and be a sharing of these diverse avenues of thought and design through the finest examples available from the submitted works. While a juried show is, by its nature, competitive, acceptance or nonacceptance follows the needs of the exhibition, and cannot be viewed as an arbiter of the final quality of a work of art.

The pool of submissions this year was stunning, and reviewing it, while initially daunting, revealed numerous patterns of shared aesthetic and conceptual explorations. Elements of painting, drawing, mixed media, watercolor, printmaking, found art, and digital art all made appearances, translated through the mediums of piecing, dyeing, sewing, and printing. References to abstract expressionism, realism, 1960s pop art, folk art, and

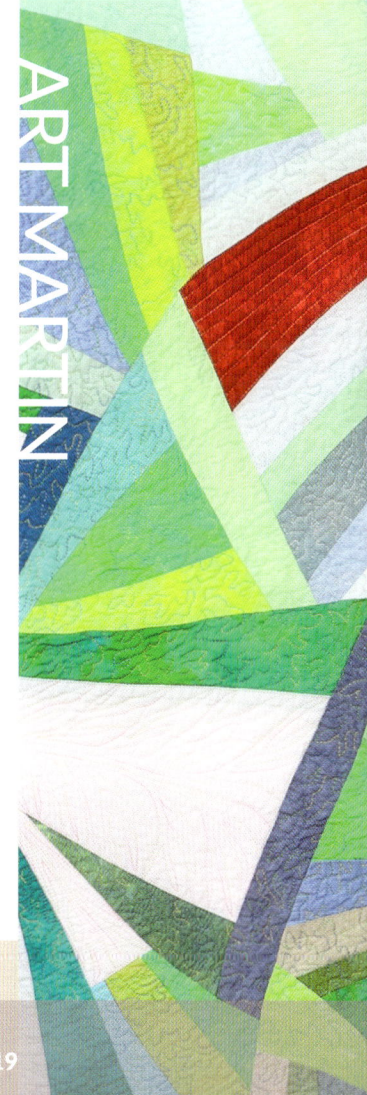

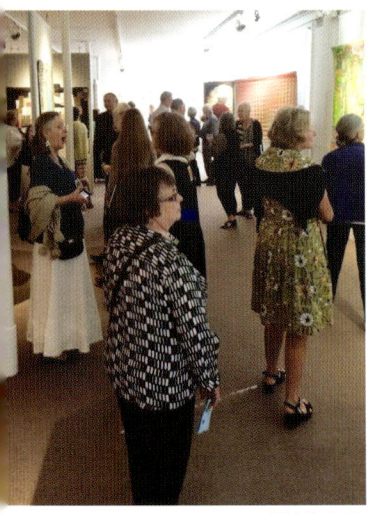

2015 Quilt National opening

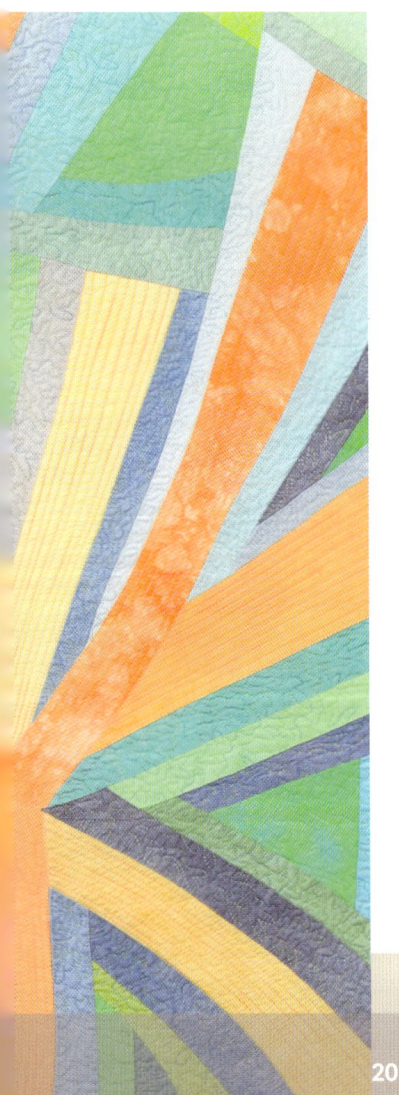

cartooning played out across the entries, accompanied by a number of conceptual and socially conscious pieces. From this blend, we singled out those artworks in the group that were visually arresting, that effectively merged the physicality of the quilting with the picture plane, and that best represented the different tracks of visual inspirations.

There was a remarkable degree of consensus between the jurors, nowhere more apparent than in our selection for Best of Show. Margaret Black's *Line Study 17* is a master statement of technique, craft, and innovative design. Black establishes a motif of a square fractured into eight sections, each shard cut by irregular concentric lines. She then repeats the square across the face of the quilt, deconstructing and reconstructing her own motif—breaking it down, changing its scale, and even rendering it solely in white pieces. The resulting rhythms, patterns, and interplay of forms are captivating.

The Quilts Japan Prize went to Denise Roberts for *Finding Connections #8*, which boasts a monochromatic ground cut through by a deceptively simple totemic green form. With no accompanying forms or patterns, precise color and design choice were paramount to executing this striking work. Liz Axford's *Shift 1* took the Award of Excellence for its masterful application of dyeing and color, creating the most atmospheric quilt in the show. Sue Benner's *Body Parts 3: Cuffed* transforms sleeve cuffs into a kaleidoscope of color and shape, elevating her source material into something new and wondrous. The intricate use of line played heavily in many of the entries, including in Judith Martin's *Soft Summer Gone*, where hand embroidery establishes mazelike patterns broken by playful, irregular circles. The skillful use of line and subtle, natural dyes made Martin's piece our winner for the Lynn Goodwin Borgman Award for Surface Design. Marina Kamenskaya presents an exuberant statement of design in pieced forms, earning her the McCarthy Memorial Award. Excitingly, a third of the artists chosen for the show this year are first-time exhibitors, making the choice for the Cathy Rasmussen Emerging Artist Memorial quite competitive. We chose *Reflections Dusk #3* by Anna Brown, for its stunning use of color and gentle, repeating and shifting patterns, a remarkable translation of the lake by her home at dusk. Finally, the three juror awards were reached only by consensus, an acknowledgement of the difficulty we faced in singling out prize recipients from such a rich field. The three pieces we chose, Karen Schulz's *...and the Skeptic*, Gertrude Spilka's *Conversations on Meaning*, and Robin Schwalb's *Born Analog* are all quite different in aesthetic and design, but share an intensely sophisticated approach to the handling of their defining visual and technical elements. Schulz brings an amazing sense of spontaneity to form and line, achieving in pieced shapes and sewn marks the effortless stroke of a painter's brush; Spilka establishes stunning monumentality through her pieced blocks, a rhythmic dance of bold red figures that tower from top to bottom of the composition; and Schwalb effectively incorporates representational imagery from a variety of sources into a cohesive narrative whole, seamlessly blending vintage images with portraiture, text, and a cartoon dinosaur.

Quilt National '17 is, in the final selections, a celebration of the spirit of the original 1979 exhibition, a declaration of the power and versatility of the quilt as a means of artistic expression. It is also a testament to the ongoing innovations and explorations of the artistic community, and the need to understand and express the world we share that drives them.

Nancy Crow

Overconnected but Finding a Little Space: Seeking Solitude #3

80" x 82"; Cotton fabrics, MX dyes; Mono-printed, machine quilted

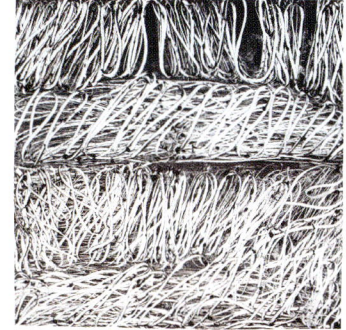

Petra Fallaux

Formations #26

83" x 85"; Hand-dyed pima cottons, Procion MX dyes; Freely cut fabric, machine pieced and quilted

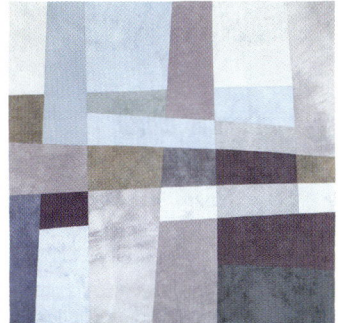

Art Martin

Cabinet Landscape: Sherman Bowling 1

15" x 17.25"; Cedar, enamel, acrylic, oil, and found object (frame and sculptural components by Lee S. Brown); Painting and woodworking, in collaboration with Lee S. Brown

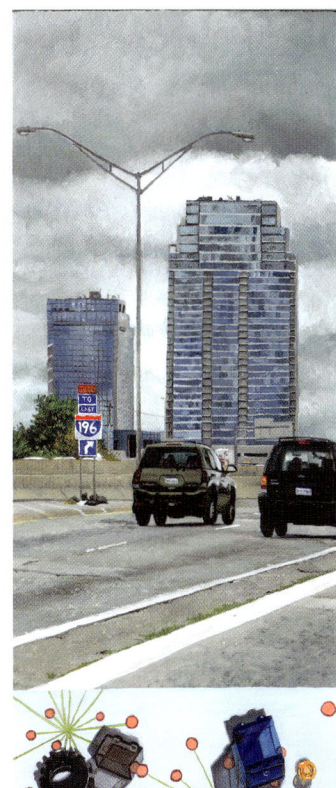

Nancy Crow, one of the *Quilt National* founders, has been making quilts for 40 years, maintaining a large studio and teaching facility on her 100-acre farm east of Columbus, Ohio. Crow was named a Fellow of the American Craft Council; she also received the National Living Treasure Award from the University of North Carolina at Wilmington. Crow is a prolific artist. She has curated and exhibited both nationally and internationally at many venues including the Renwick Gallery of the Smithsonian Institution, the Museum of Arts and Design in New York City, the Cultural Arts Museum of Konstanz, Germany, and among many others, the Auckland Art Museum, New Zealand.

Petra Fallaux is a writer, curator, creative director, and artist. In addition to helping direct Springboard Design, an award-winning architectural firm, Fallaux is an active studio artist whose primary focus since 2003 is to make one-of-a-kind quilts. After receiving degrees from the Universities of Leiden and Amsterdam in Psychology and Film Studies, she went on to earn a Master of Arts Management degree from Carnegie Mellon University and directed its university art galleries for over 10 years. During her tenure she founded and guided the building of the 10,000-square-foot Miller Gallery and curated more than 100 exhibitions in a variety of media ranging from paintings, prints, and drawings to architecture, video, design, and site-specific installations.

Art Martin is the Associate Curator/Collections Manager at the Muskegon Museum of Art. He is the organizing curator for several recent international fiber exhibitions, including the traveling exhibitions *Innovators and Legends: Generations in Textiles and Fibers* and *Extreme Fibers: Textile Icons and the New Edge* with guest curator Geary Jones, and the upcoming *Circular Abstractions: Bull's Eye Quilts* with guest curator Nancy Crow. A practicing artist, Martin holds a BFA in Painting and Drawing from Drake University and a MFA in Painting from Wichita State University.

JUROR BIOS

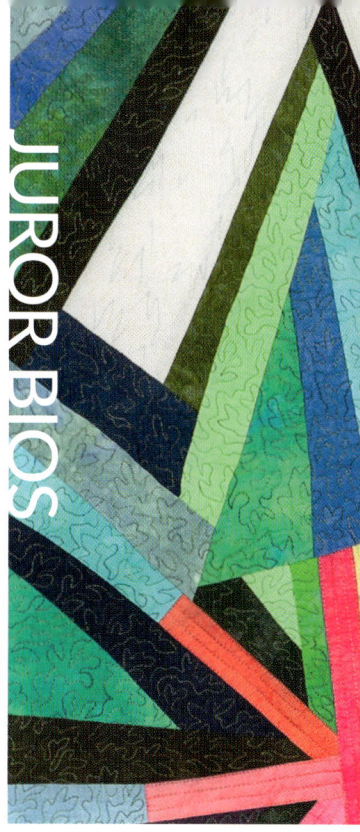

For many years I heard quilt artists talking about Quilt National *and the Dairy Barn, but I didn't know what it was all about. Then I attended my first* Quilt National, *and was blown away! This biennial exhibition of art quilts attracts top collectors from around the country, and serves as an incubator for new ideas in fiber art.*

– *Luana Rubin, founder of Equilter.com*

PRIZE
QUILTS

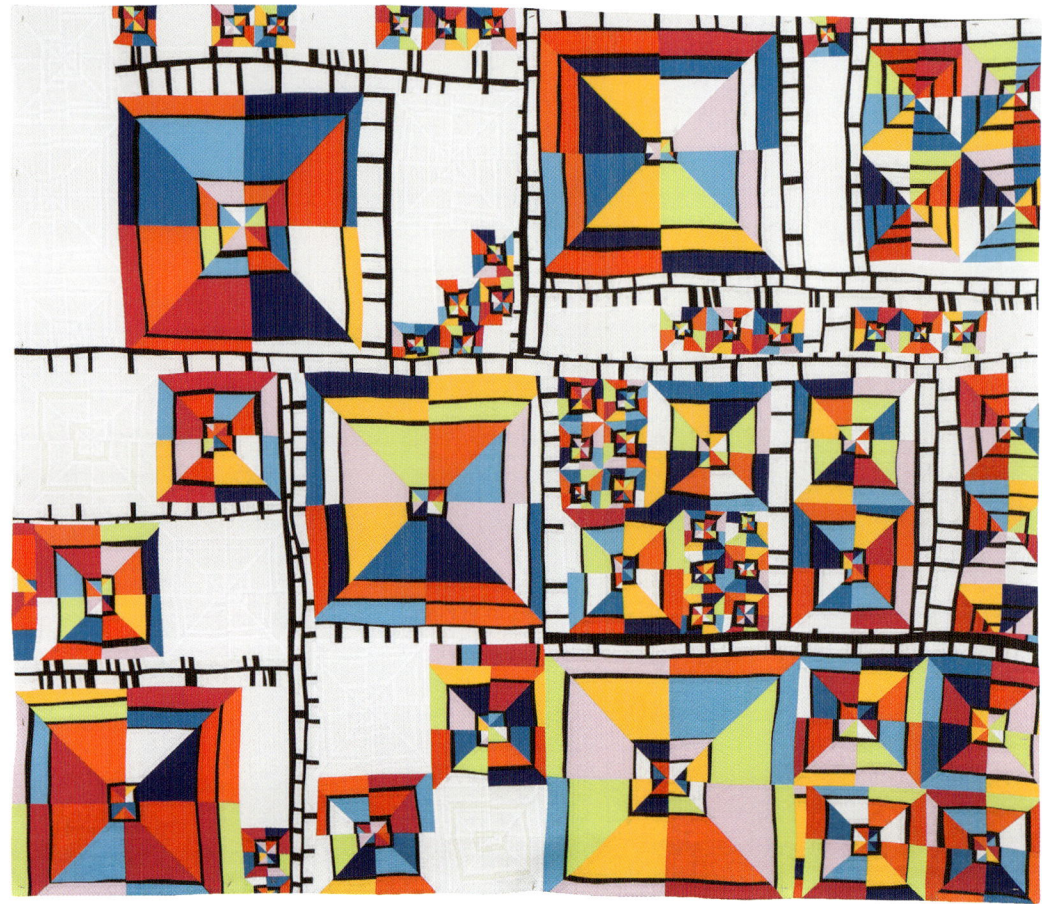

MARGARET BLACK
Boswell, Pennsylvania

Line Study 17
90″ x 75″

Kona cottons, thread, wool batting, cotton batting

Free-form cut and pieced, straight-line machine quilted

I make art using fabric which is free-form cut and pieced. Line Study 17 is part of my body of work that explores line and color. I like my art to be energetic and joyful so that it delivers happiness to the viewer. I consider the final stitches and threads to be my paintbrush that adds surface design and texture to the piece.

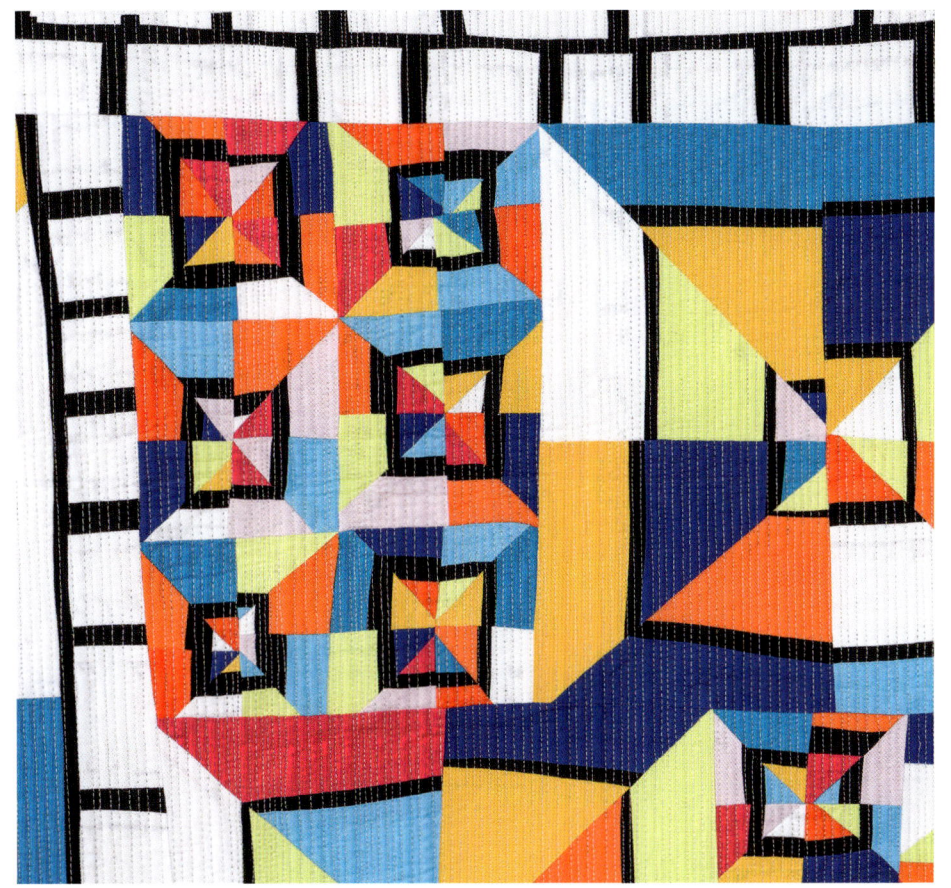

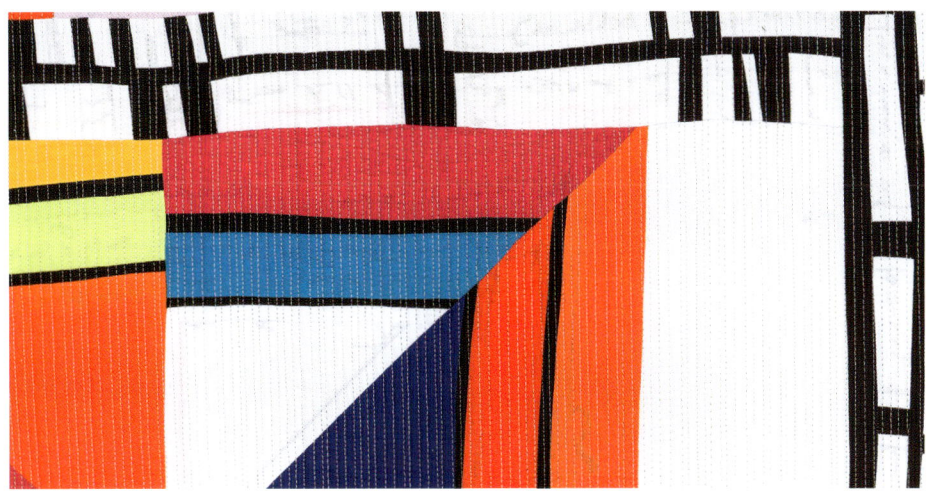

Line Study 17
(detail)

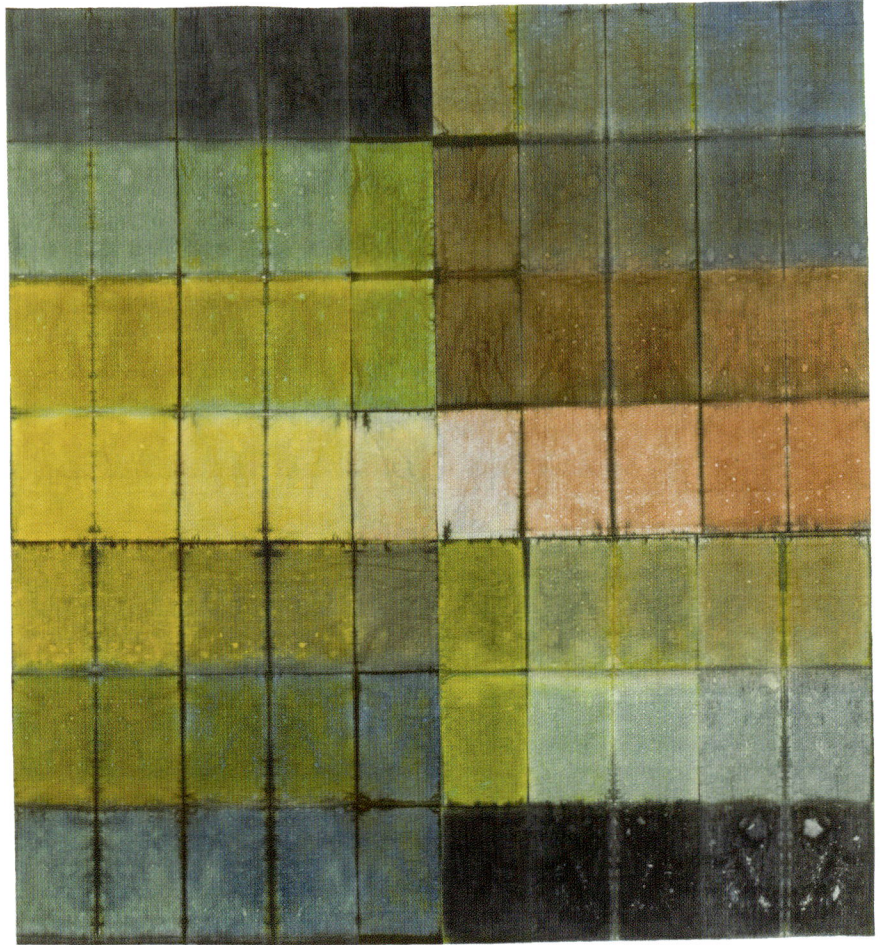

LIZ AXFORD
Clinton, Washington

Shift 1
75" x 69"

Hand-dyed cotton broadcloth, cotton batting, cotton threads

Resist dyed, machine pieced and quilted

The combination of repeated geometric forms and the possibility for infinite variation within that repetition is what first attracted me to quilt making as an art form. Working with my hand-dyed fabrics affords me the opportunity to combine painterly effects with hard-edged geometry.

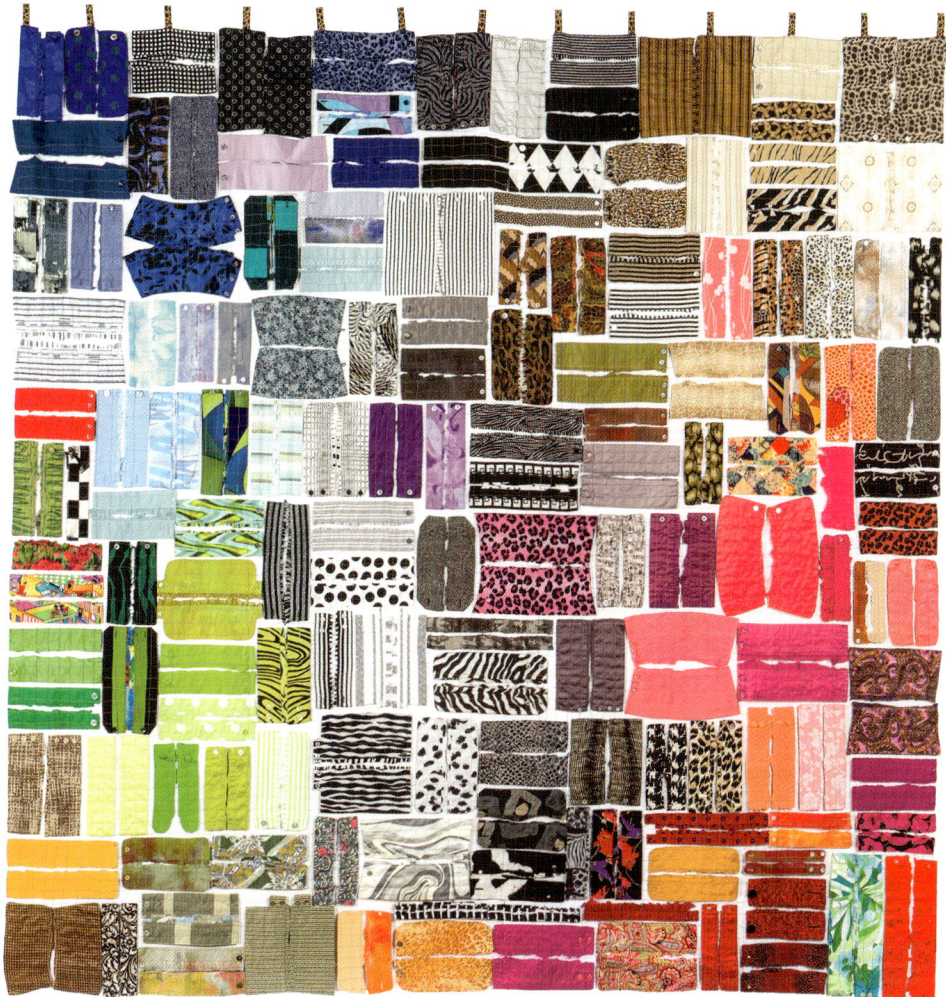

SUE BENNER
Dallas, Texas

Body Parts 3: Cuffed
90″ x 89″

Cuffs (silk, polyester, interfacing, buttons), thread

Machine stitched and quilted, some cuffs are dyed

Collecting and recycling women's fashion has been a part of my studio work for over 20 years. In the continuation of this series, I am examining the concept of quilt to consider ready-made objects that already exist with three layers. These blouses and dresses have sacrificed their cuffs for this work and I am in their debt.

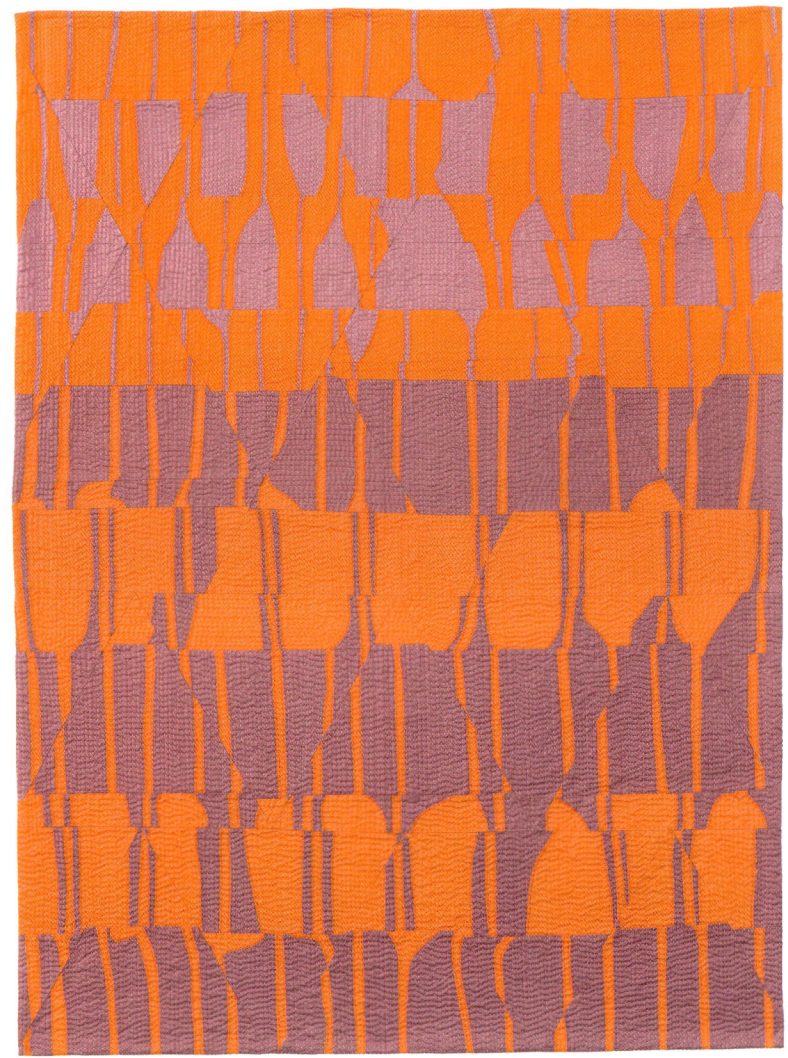

ANNA BROWN
Bungwahl, New South Wales, Australia

REFLECTIONS Dusk #3
49" x 37"

Commercial cotton fabric, cotton thread, synthetic batting

Machine pieced, raw edge appliquéd, hand quilted

I work from my home studio in the Great Lakes area of New South Wales, Australia. My main source of inspiration comes from my immediate environment, the local bushland, and lakes. I love creating contemporary art quilts while still incorporating some traditional techniques.

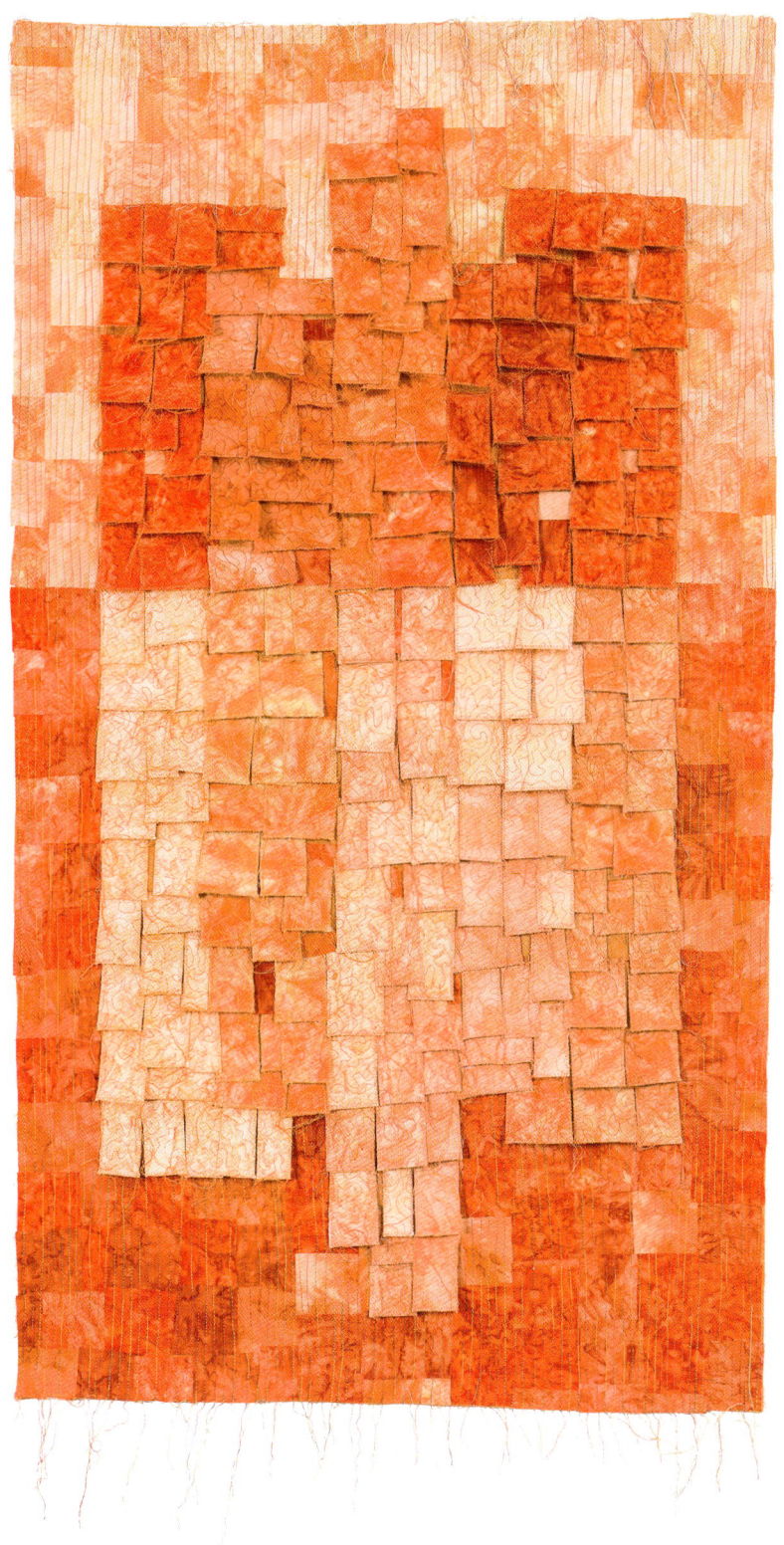

ETI DAVID
Ramat Hasharon,
Israel

Orange Towers
50″ x 30″

Commercial cotton
fabrics, polyester
batting, various threads

Machine pieced
and quilted, three
dimensional pieces
hanging from
the quilt surface

*I was intrigued with
using only one fabric
for a whole quilt. I found
that the batik-gradated
fabric gave me the
answer for my wish.*

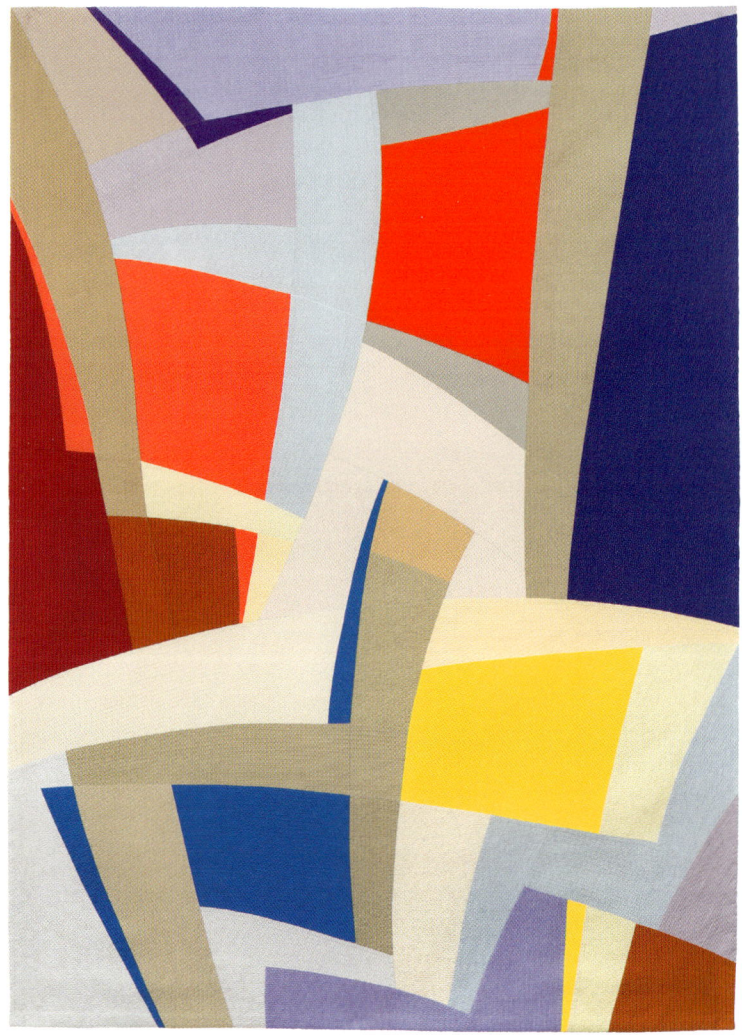

MARINA KAMENSKAYA
Wauconda, Illinois

Squares #1: Red, Yellow, Blue
68″ x 50″

Cotton fabrics

Machine pieced and quilted

I explore line, shape, color, balance, movement, tension and texture. I follow my chosen medium and its innate qualities and possibilities. Every next work takes on from where the previous one has ended. I have my own vision as an artist, but like any artist I cannot make anyone see what I see. I can only speak with my own voice and let it be heard. Art does not require explanation.

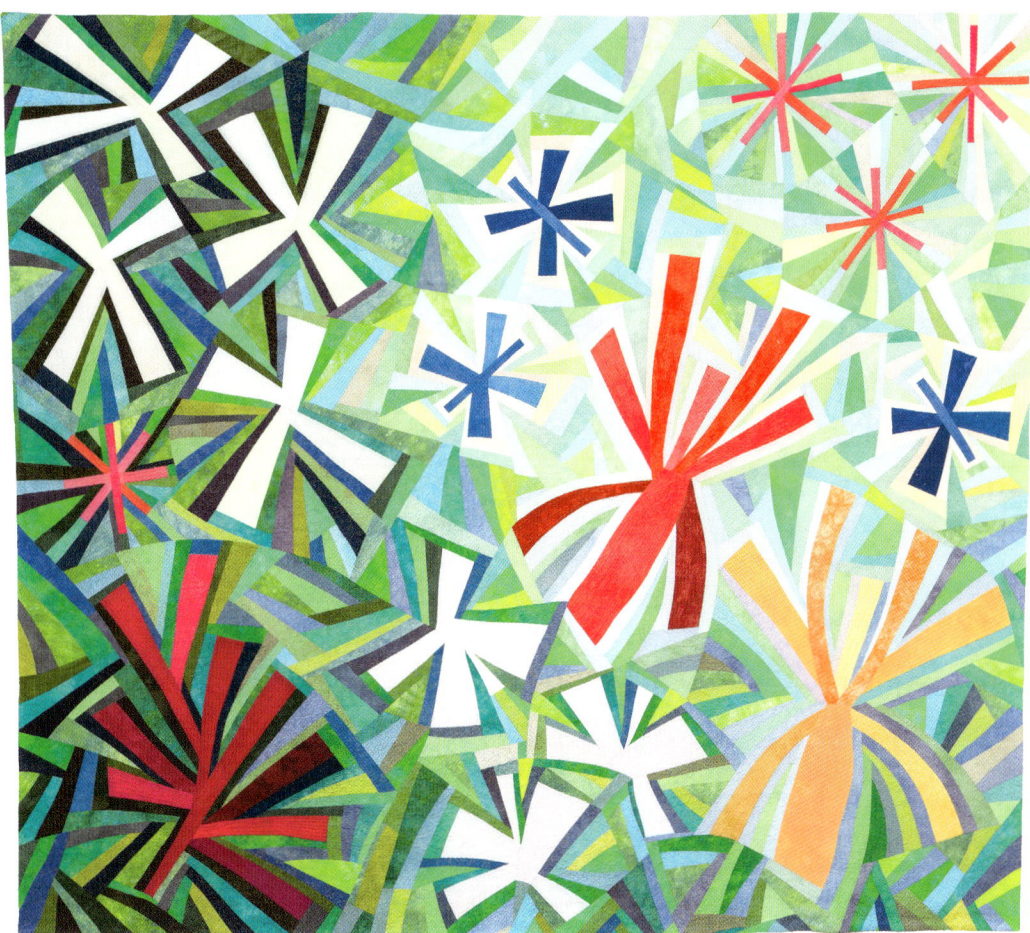

PAMELA LOEWEN
Williamston, Michigan

Butterfly Garden
82″ x 92″

Hand-dyed cotton fabrics, wool batting

Free-form cut, machine pieced and free-motion quilted

The natural world inspires me. Plants especially intrigue me with an almost infinite variety of configurations—branches, stems, leaves, flowers—each species has its unique forms. A garden is cultivated growth, nourished beauty. My garden series explores the themes of growth and beauty in a variety of contexts. Butterfly Garden, thirteenth in this series, explores growth in the midst of light and shadow.

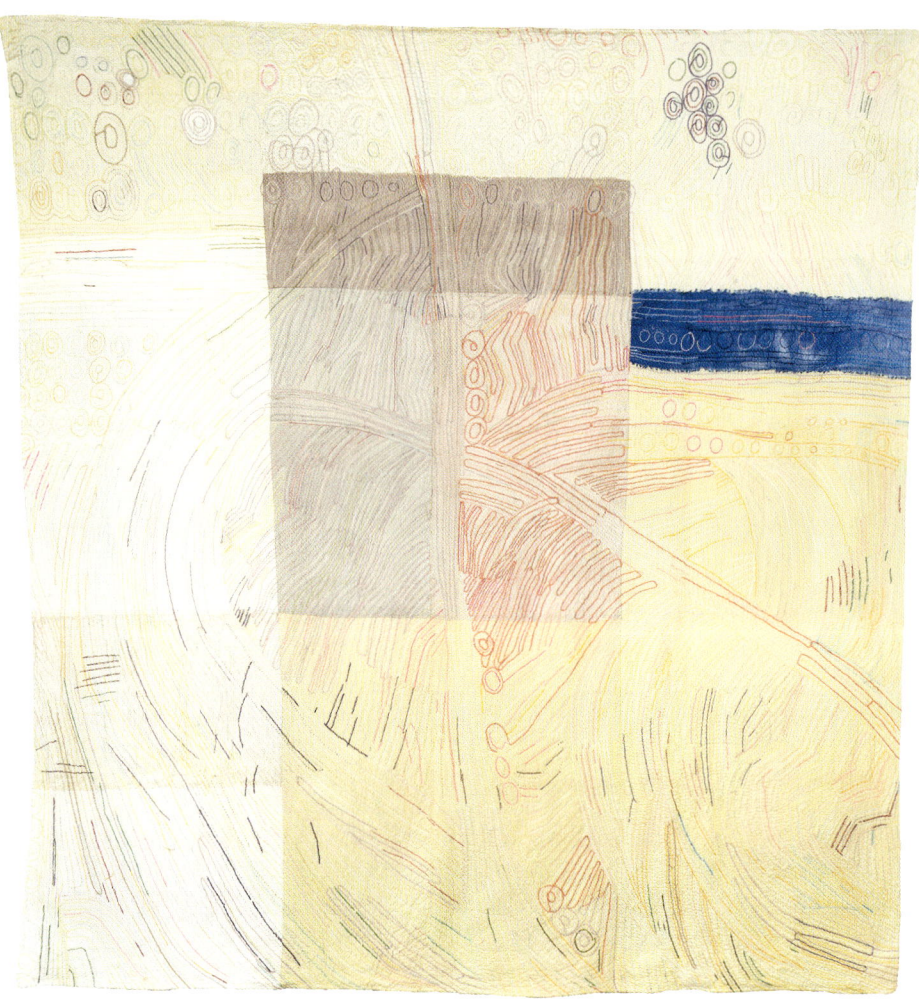

JUDITH E. MARTIN
Sheguiandah, Ontario, Canada

Soft Summer Gone
100″ x 100″

Plant-dyed silk, silk floss, wool yarn, wool batting, silk chiffon backing

Dyed, layered, hand pieced, embroidered, and quilted

*Small marks/large emptiness. Working slowly and in
solitude with a hoop, it feels as if I have the land in my lap.*

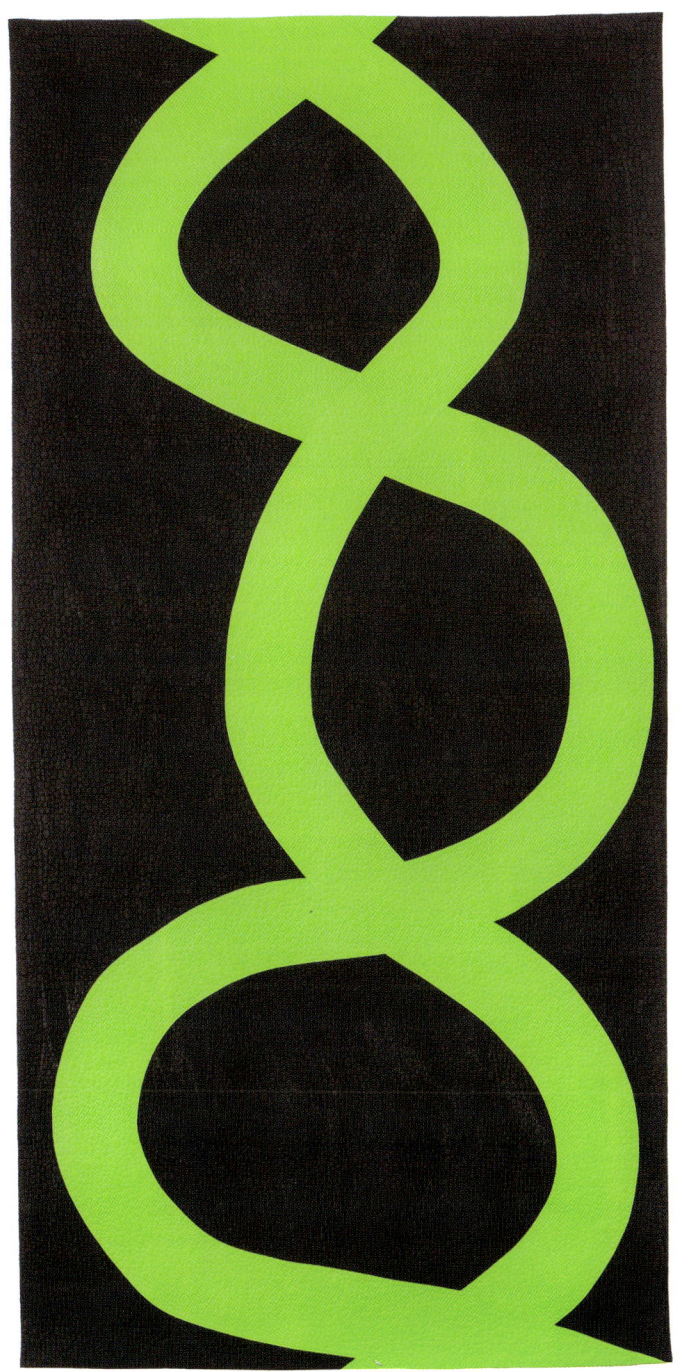

DENISE L. ROBERTS
Albright, West Virginia

Finding Connections #8
42″ x 84.5″

Hand-dyed cotton fabric, cotton batting, thread, commercial cotton fabric

Direct fabric cuts, machine pieced and quilted

After years of creating very complex work, I have a desire to explore spare compositions. This figure was created using two curvilinear shapes. Once joined they created connections to form this figure. This new figure resembles some kind of character to me, a being. As I create more of these characters in this new series, I think of them all hung together finding connections to each other as human beings do daily in their lives.

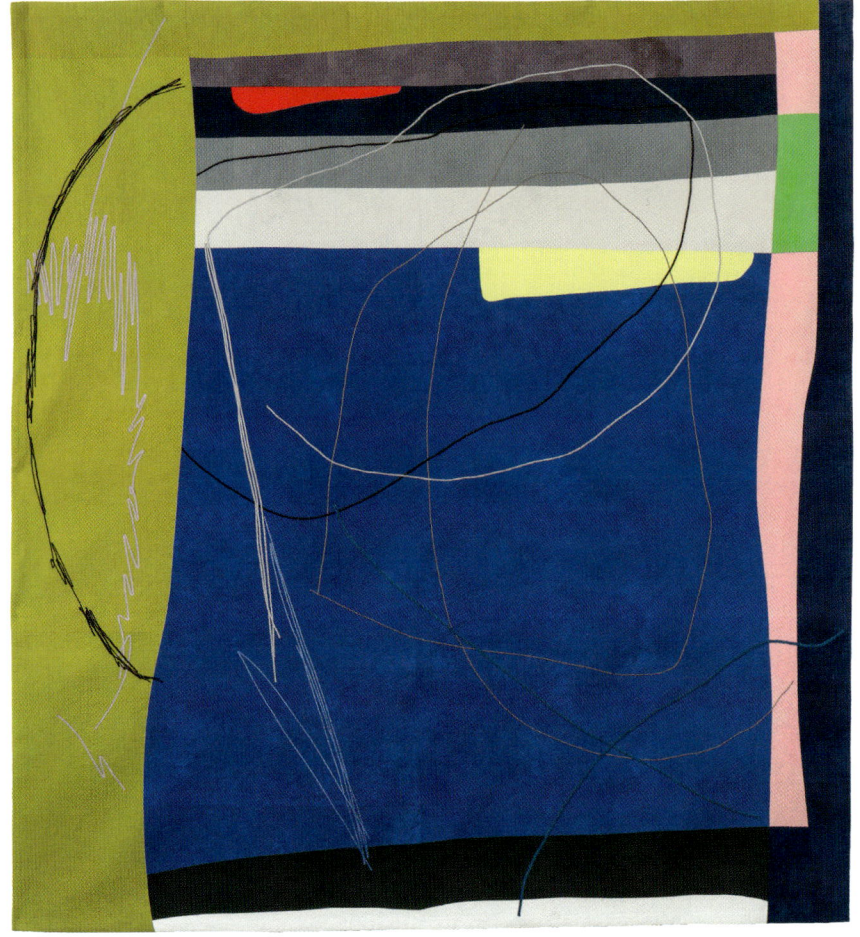

KAREN SCHULZ
Silver Spring, Maryland

...and the Skeptic
81″ x 76″

Cotton fabric, cotton batting, thread, yarn

Hand dyed, machine pieced, free-motion machine quilted, couched

This piece is the result of a sketch made after a five-hour visit to the Art Institute of Chicago. I was so taken with the sheer breadth of everything I had seen. I found myself asking the question, "What are you afraid of?" The answer came back, "Look at what people have done. You can do anything." I decided then and there to embrace the whole of myself, the poet and the skeptic.

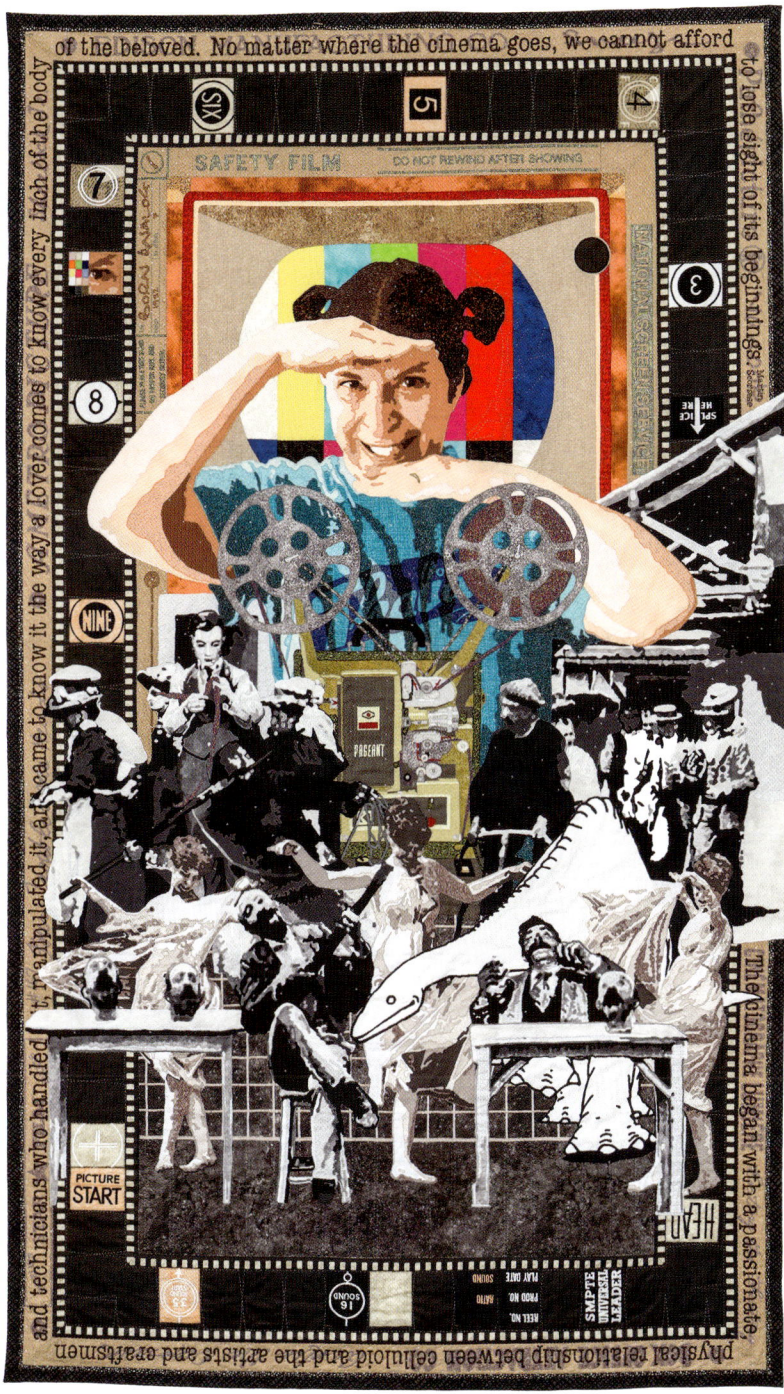

ROBIN SCHWALB
Brooklyn, New York

Born Analog
80" x 47"

Silk-screened and commercially available cotton fabrics, thread

Fused, machine appliquéd, hand appliquéd, machine pieced, hand quilted

Gertie is a dinosaur because she was drawn that way by animator Windsor McKay. I'm a dinosaur because, in this increasingly digital and digitized age, I'm still licensed by the City of New York to run 35mm motion picture film. Here I celebrate classic works of proto- and early cinema by Muybridge, the Lumière brothers, Georges Méliès, Edison, Buster Keaton, and Robert Flaherty, as well as my own history as a film projectionist.

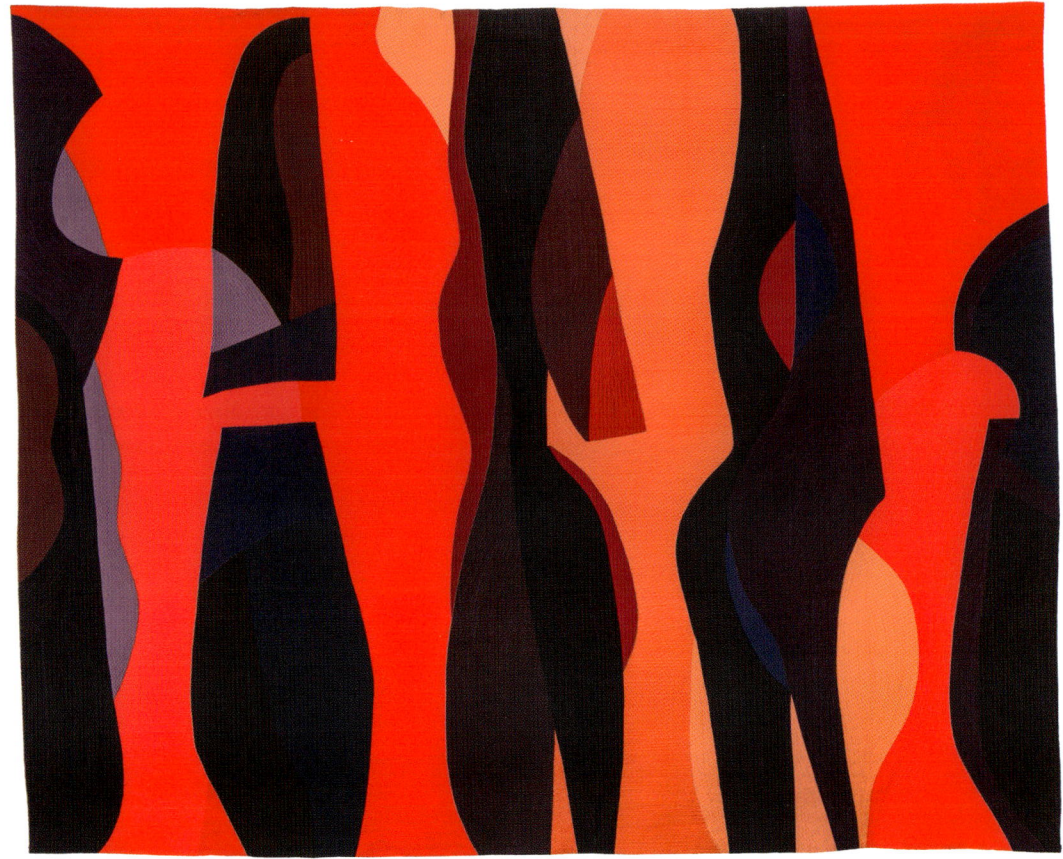

GERRI SPILKA
Philadelphia, Pennsylvania

Conversations on Meaning
82″ x 100″

Commercial and hand-dyed cottons, cotton batting, wool batting, cotton thread

Improvisationally machine pieced and quilted, denoted by artist,
machine quilted by Marina Baudoin

This piece is part of my Interactions series, which reflects a fascination with a recurrent set of themes that have reappeared in all my life's work: the interactions, relationships, and ambiguities inherent among people, place, and human-made and biological forces. In my artwork, these are expressed through two dimensional shapes, negative spaces, straight and curved lines, colors, and subtle texture. This is not surprising, as I am trained in this order: as an artist, social scientist, and architect and urban planner.

THE QUILTS

Quilt National *is the most prestigious display of art quilts in the US. Entry has been a part of my studio work for the past 10 years. The quilts that did not get juried in for the early years are still part of my solo exhibits and get accepted into other Midwest art shows. I have been privileged to exhibit with Quilt National '15 and '17.*

— *Daren Redman, artist*

NATALYA AIKENS

Pleasantville,
New York

Iron Spine 5XL
77″ x 51″

Vintage linen,
repurposed plastic
bags, repurposed
plastic drop cloth,
rayon, cotton, snow-
dyed pine thread,
vintage lace, dyed
dryer sheets

Collaged, freehand
machine embroidered,
hand stitched

*I celebrate the beauty
of architecture
around me and stitch
skyscrapers, buildings,
homes, bridges, and fire
escapes. Reclaimed and
repurposed materials
such as vintage linens,
fabric scraps, and plastic
shopping bags are in my
paint box. I collage and
layer, sketch, and stitch
by hand and machine. I
use my sewing machine
for thread sketching and
then spend many hours
of hand stitching on all
the intimate details.*

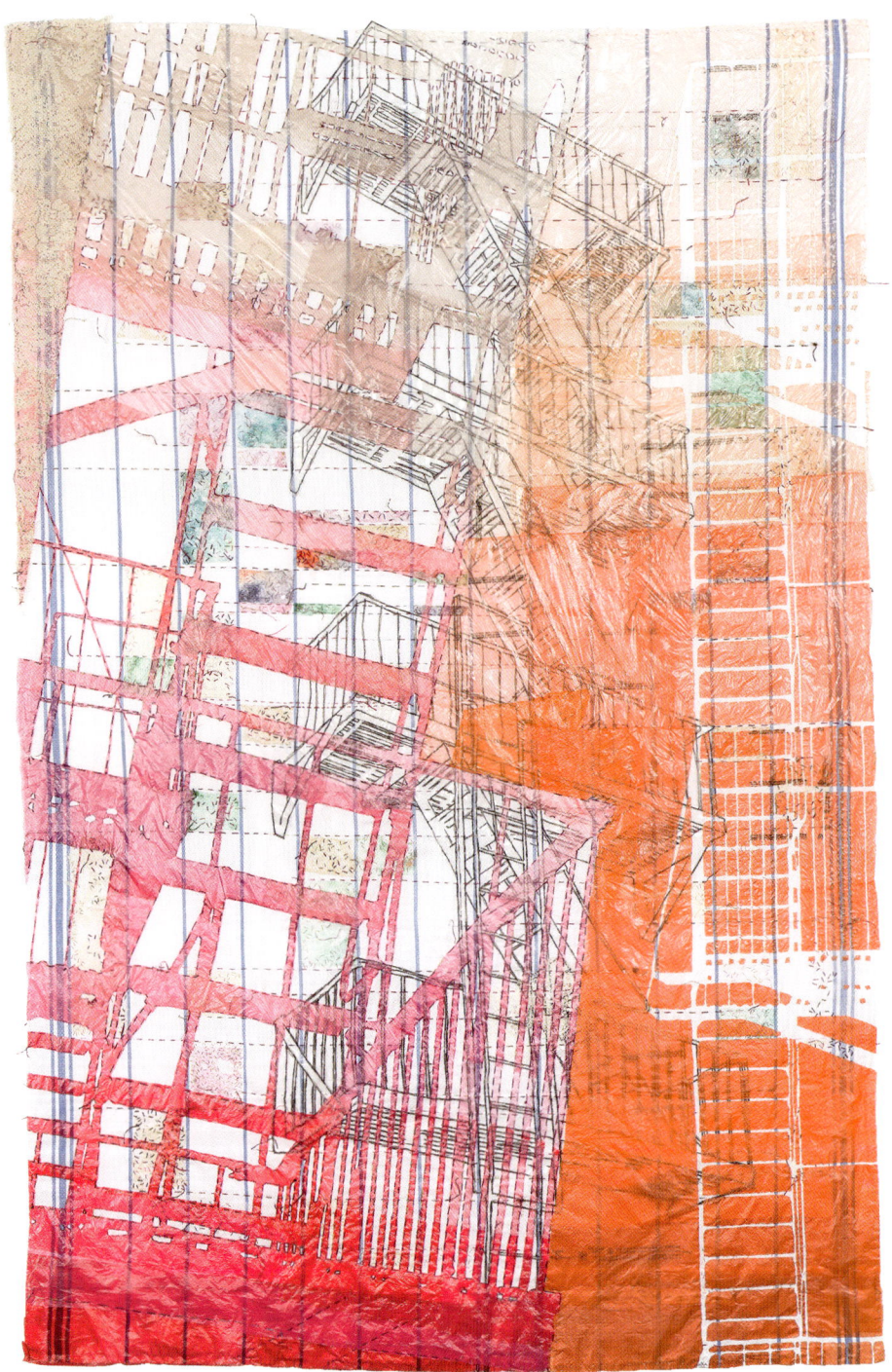

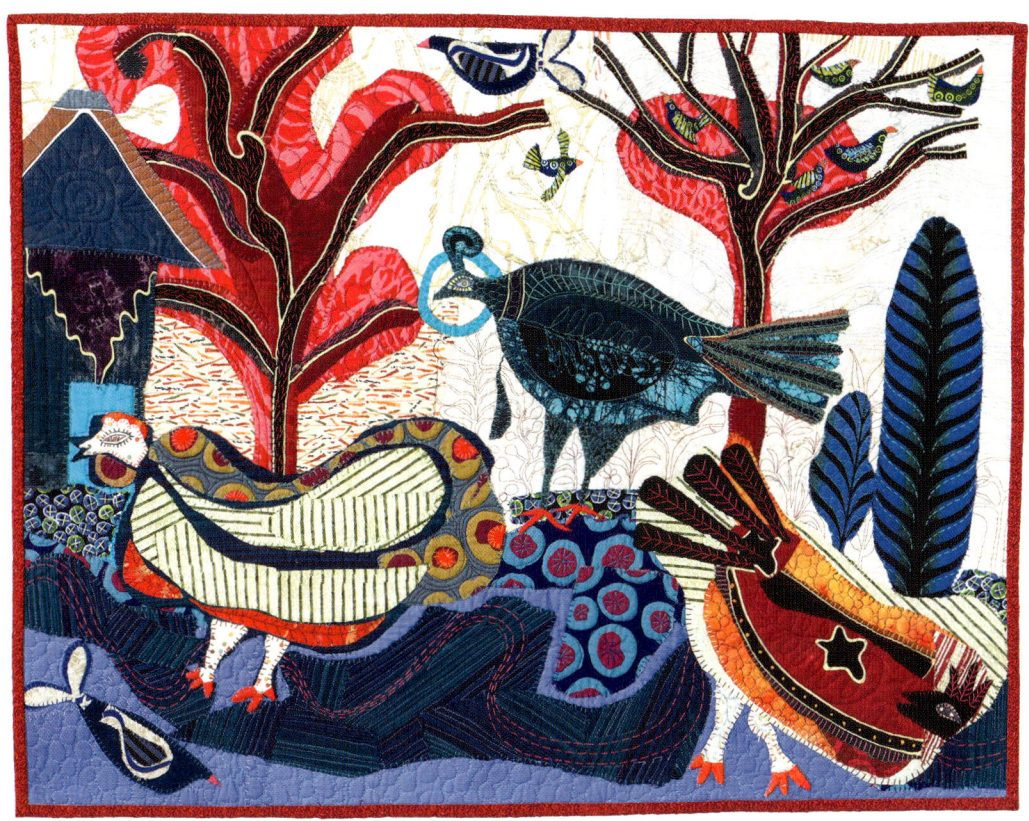

PAMELA ALLEN
Kingston, Ontario, Canada

11 Birds—3 Domestic, 8 Wild
35″ x 44″

Recycled and commercial fabric,
computer-printed fabric eyes

Hand raw-edge appliquéd, machine
free-motion quilted, hand topstitched

*This quilt commemorates the turkey in the scene. It gave
its life so as to make a permanent dent in our brand
new car the first day we drove it. May it rest in peace.*

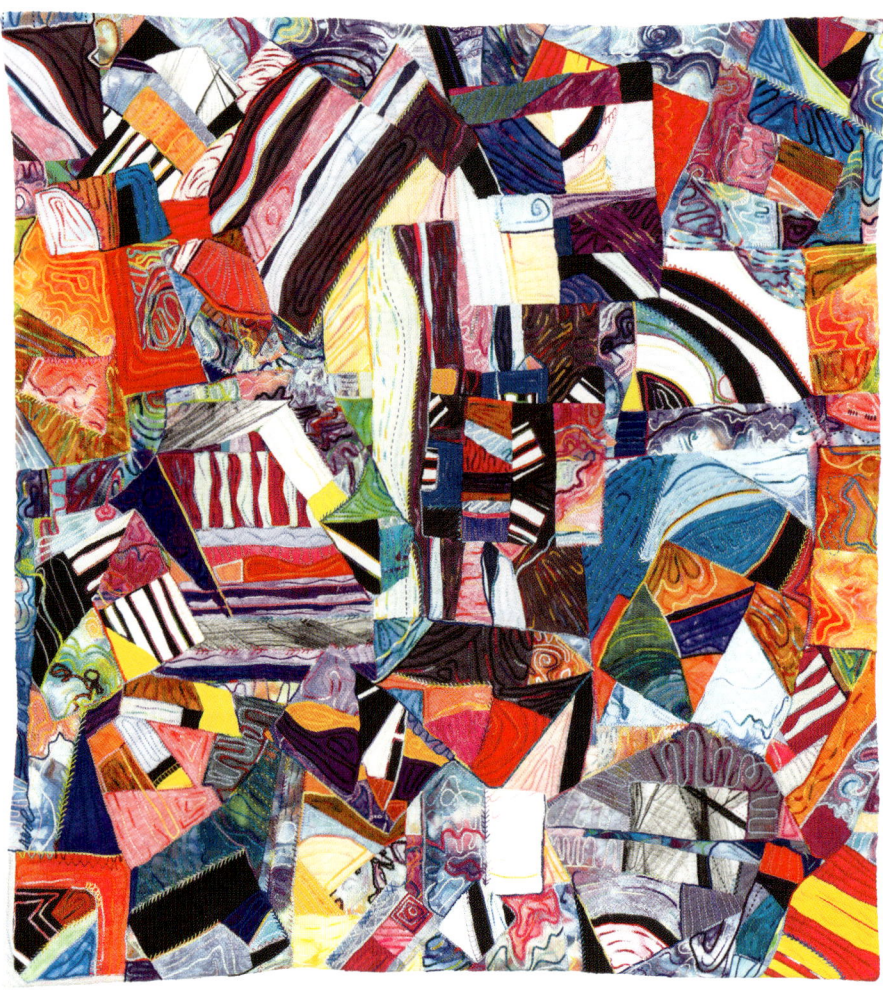

SANDRA ALTENBERG
Anacortes, Washington

Walk into My Textural Scribblings
27″ x 29″

Hand-dyed cotton fabric, commercial cotton fabric, painted cotton fabric, cotton batting, lace weight hand-dyed cotton, silk, and wool yarn, commercial cotton thread, embroidery thread

Pieced, machine quilted, hand embroidered

Trusting my own instincts to produce expressive art is a constant struggle. I strive toward a rhythm and freshness, feeling the composition and the emotion of the color as I proceed with the power of the field stitching uniting into focus.

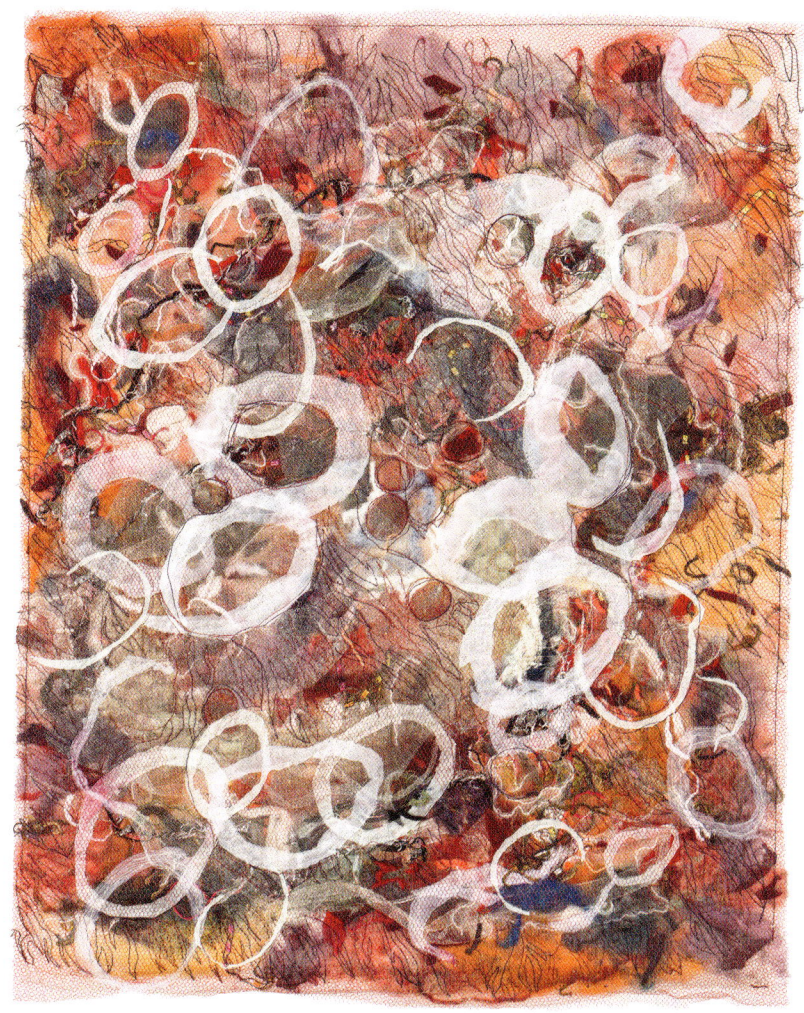

COLLEEN ANSBAUGH
Manitowoc, Wisconsin

Hot Sugar Cells
30″ x 24″

Raw wool, non-woven fabric, netting, silk,
various yarns and threads, nylon, glitter

Hand-dyed raw wool stitched and layered with various yarns
and fabrics sandwiched between netting, machine stitched

*Good or bad, blood runs through our veins. Sugar, while sweet tasting,
can really be deadly. Some people need medicine to control sugar
spikes. Once in the tummy, how is sugar controlled? Is there such a
thing as sugar police? With my sweet tooth, I may be headed for trouble.*

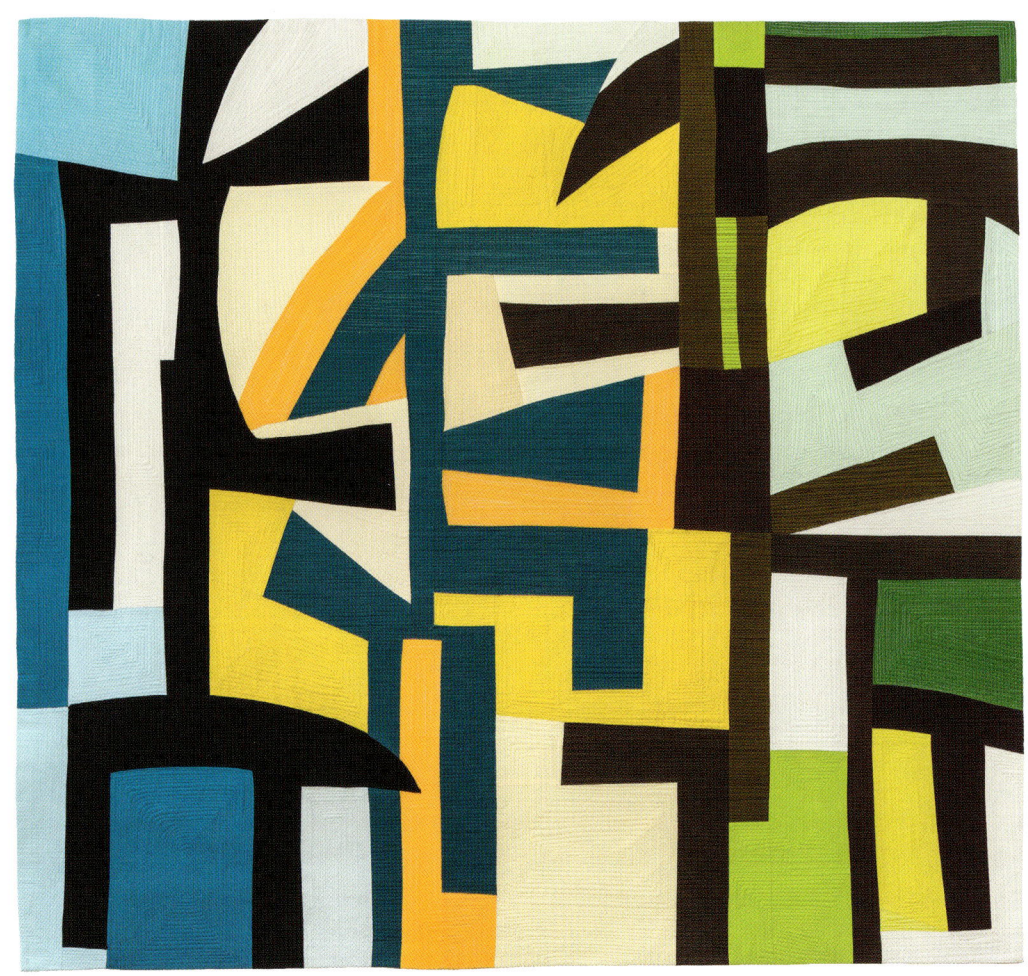

CATHERINE BEARD
Springfield, Oregon

Aizuchi
60″ x 55.5″

Hand-dyed and commercial cotton fabrics, wool batting

Pieced

*The art of conversation and personal interaction seem at a
premium in the tech-driven world we share. This work is a reminder
of the importance of face-to-face dialogue in its many forms.*

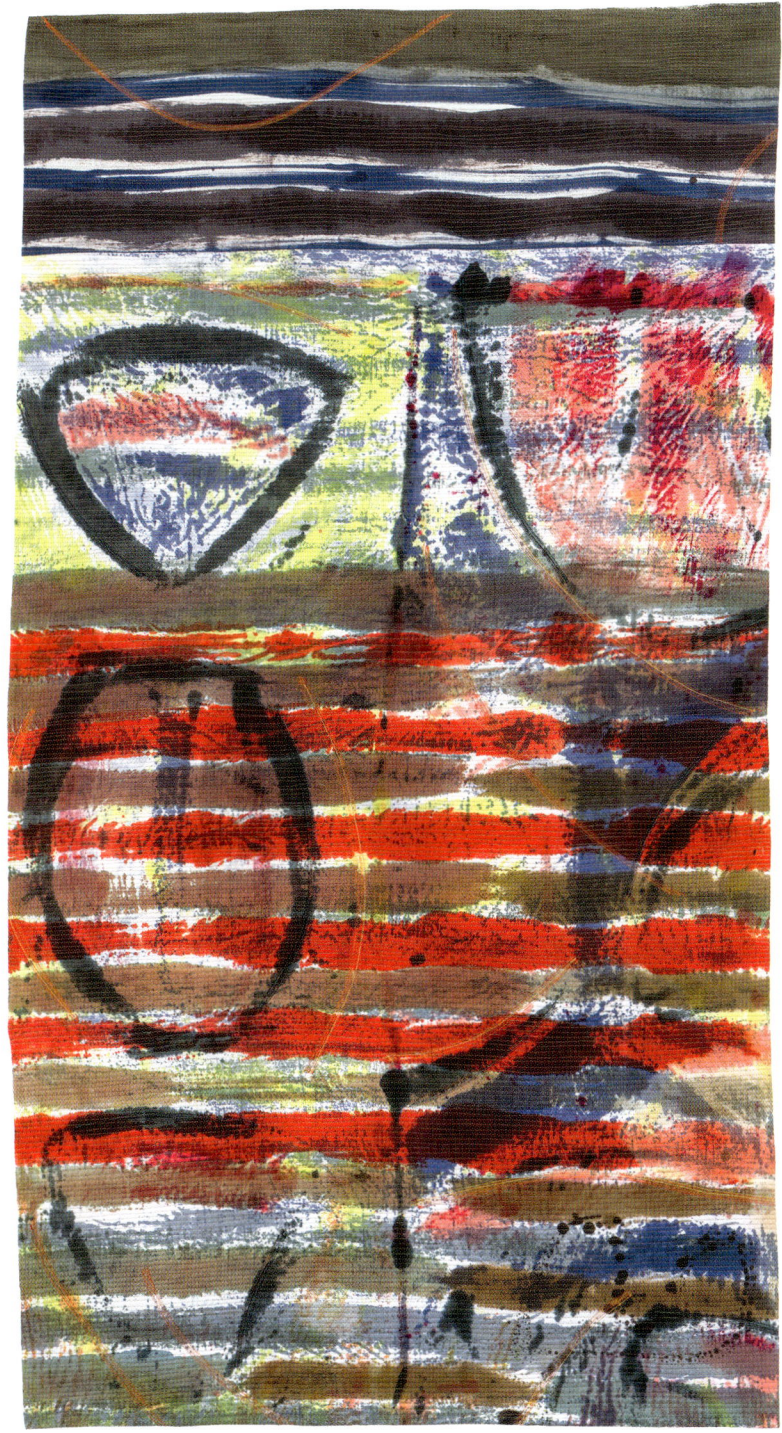

ASTRID HILGER BENNETT
Iowa City, Iowa

Ways of Seeing: Water
63″ x 35″

Cotton fabric, cotton batting, Procion fiber reactive dyes, regular and Sulky threads

Hand painted and mono-printed using thickened fiber reactive dyes, machine stitched

I'm happiest with a brush in my hand. Art quilts allow me a large-scale, exuberant canvas. Music, visual mark-making, the natural world, and the emotive effect of color all figure into my work. What appears to be abstract is actually the sum of all life experiences. Stitching is a vital part of the language of this piece, integrating all layers to a much greater extent than I usually do. For this reason, I chose to let the drape of the textile mimic the sense of water as a visual layer.

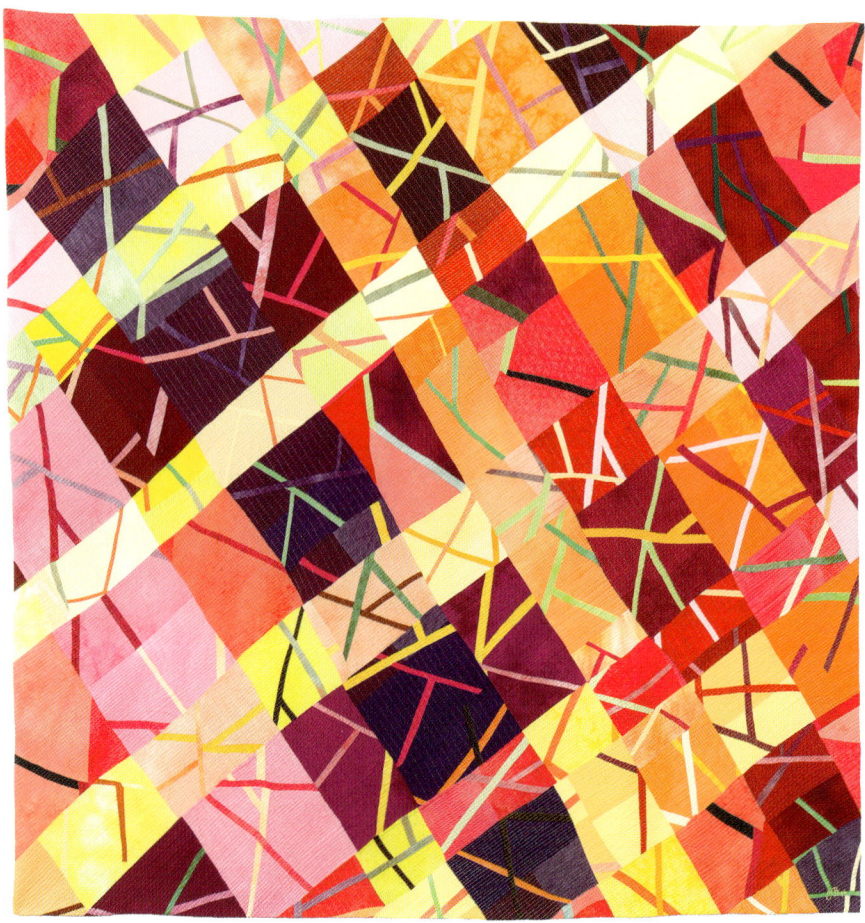

EDITH BIERI-HANSELMANN
Neftenbach, Switzerland

Fury & Despair
80″ x 80″

Hand-dyed cotton fabric, cotton linen blend,
commercial cotton embroidery thread

Machine pieced and quilted

*Quilting is my big passion. I love to play with colors and forms. With my art
I simply want to give joy and good feelings. I love to sew and quilt with my
sewing machine and also use mostly self-dyed fabrics. While making this
quilt I had to go through a very tough time; therefore, this might be a strange
name. But the energy it sends out has been a big help to me while making it.*

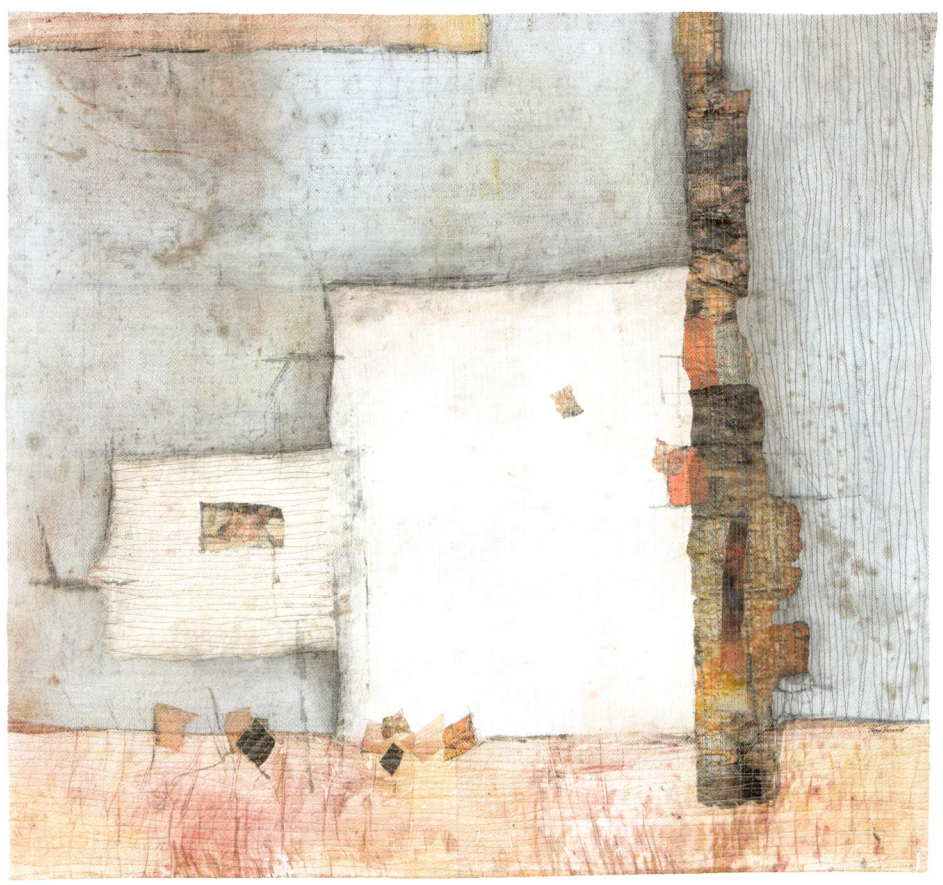

PEGGY BROWN
Nashville, Indiana

Passageway
39″ x 43″

Silk, archival tissue paper protected by acrylic matte medium, transparent watercolor paint, digital transfer from a section of one of my paintings, thread, cotton batting, cotton fabric

Hand painted, collaged, hand quilted

I approach my work from the viewpoint of a watercolor artist and use the same medium and methods to paint on fabric that I have used for years when painting on paper. Earthy colors and numerous, often secretive, passageways with their crumbling rock-surrounds intrigued me during a trip to Tuscany, Italy. Passageway is an abstract translation of my fascination with those textures, shapes, and hues.

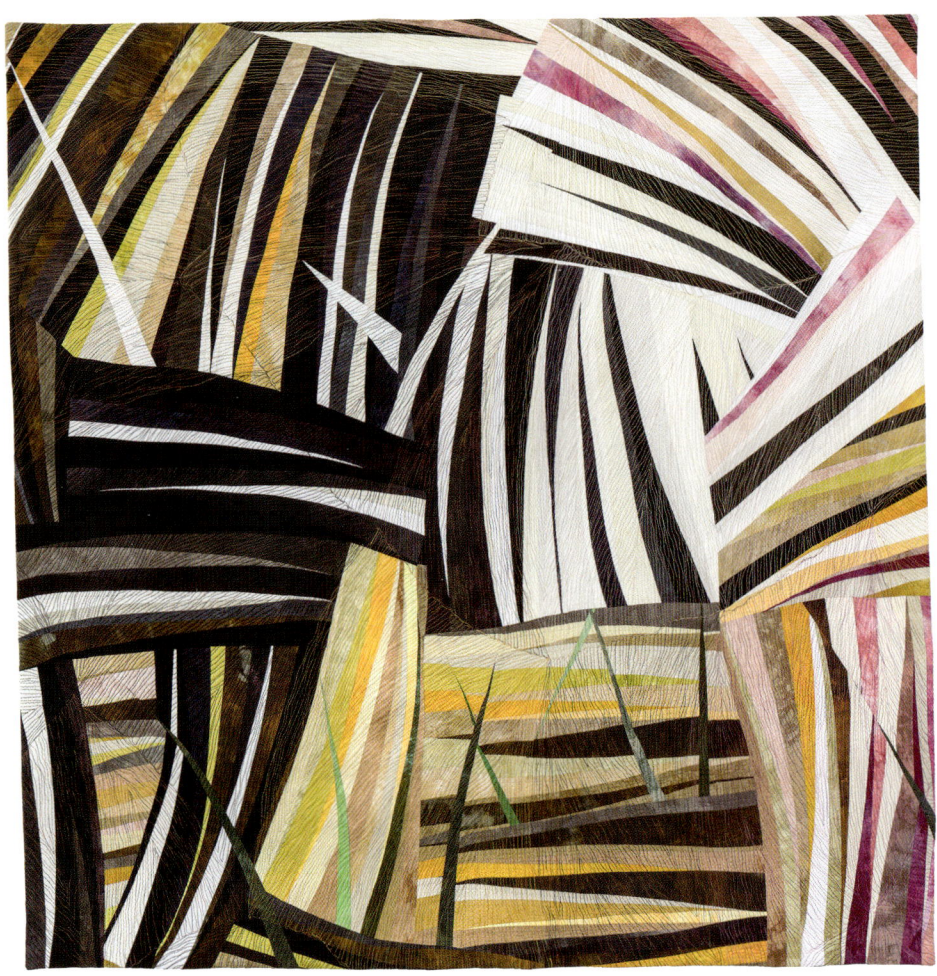

BONNIE BUCKNAM
Vancouver, Washington

Zebra
51″ x 51″

Hand-dyed cotton fabric

Machine pieced and quilted

While touring South Africa, I had the pleasure of seeing a zebra in the wild. Their geometric stripes contrast with the naturally dry veldt and the grassy mountain terrain.

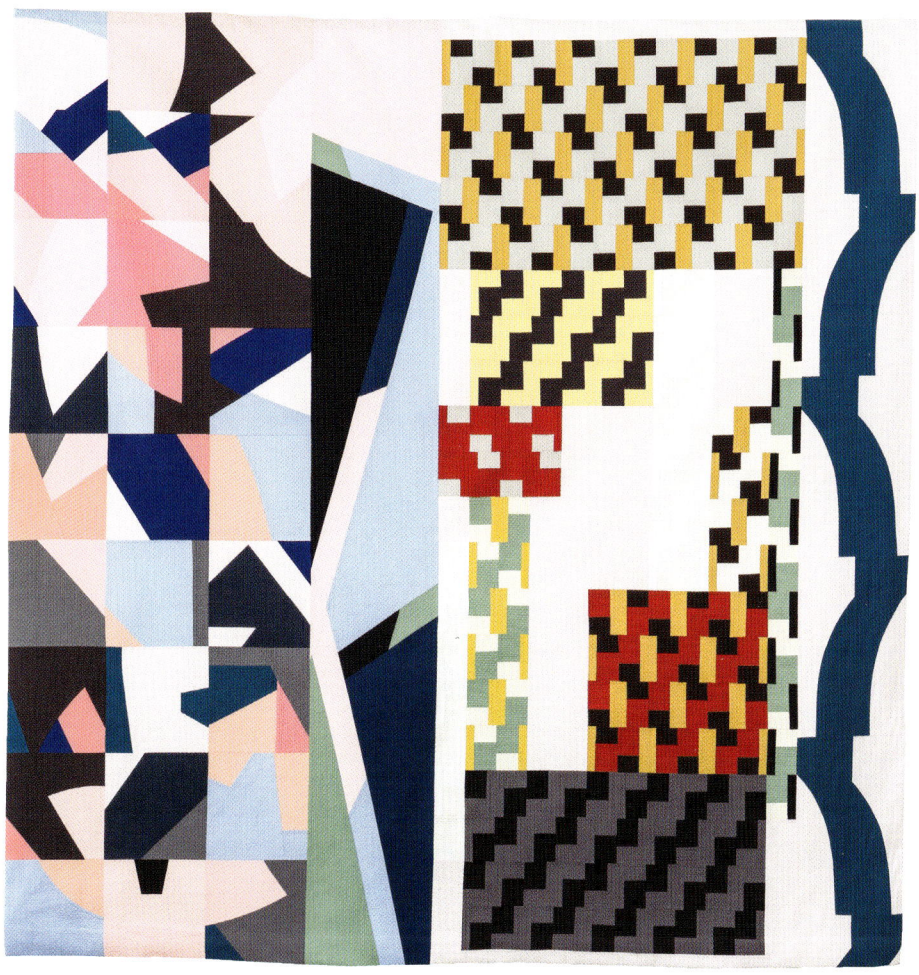

PAT BUDGE
Garden Valley, Idaho

Last Rites
82″ x 79″

Cotton commercial fabric, batting, thread

Freehand and precision cut, machine pieced, and quilted

I don't know the last time I had a lucid moment with my father. It might have been a week before he died from Alzheimer's disease, a shell of a mind within the body of an athlete. Or maybe it was years earlier as his garbled words became the norm. Maybe it was recognition I saw in his eyes as I held his hand at the last, but, in reality, I don't know.

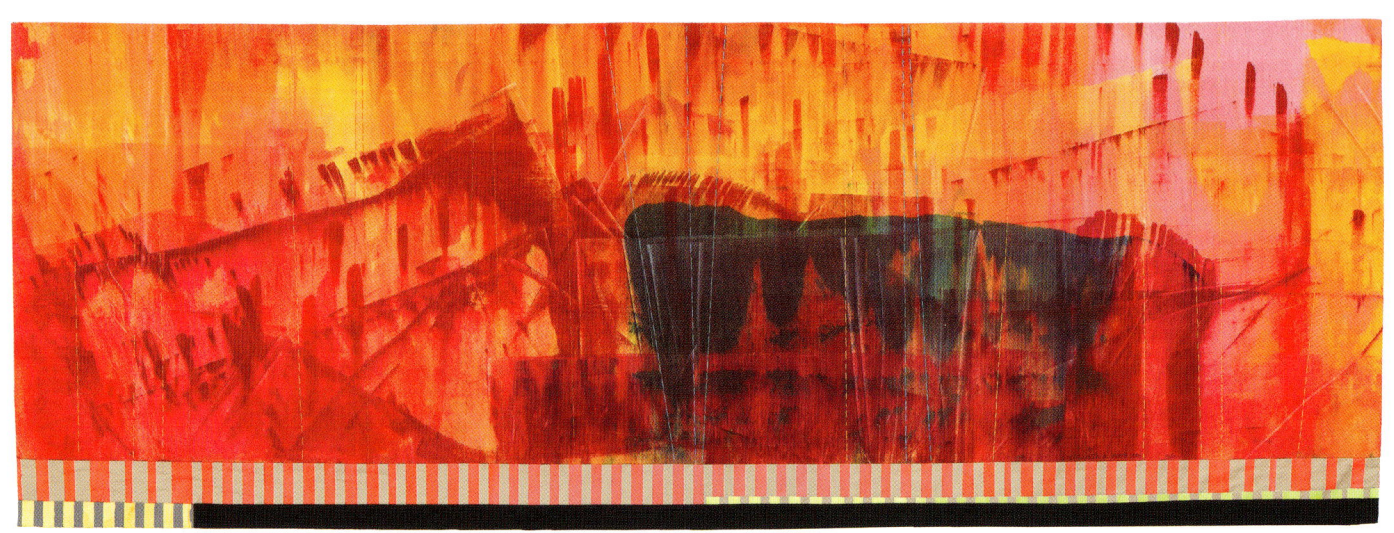

ELIZABETH BUSCH
Glenburn, Maine

Fire in the Belly
24″ x 66″

Cotton canvas, textile paints, commercial fabric, polyester batting, cotton back, embroidery floss

Hand painted, machine pieced, hand quilted

"Fire in the belly ... a spark of the divine ... a dormant volcano," the choice to show up for my work to "delightfully and abundantly" create!

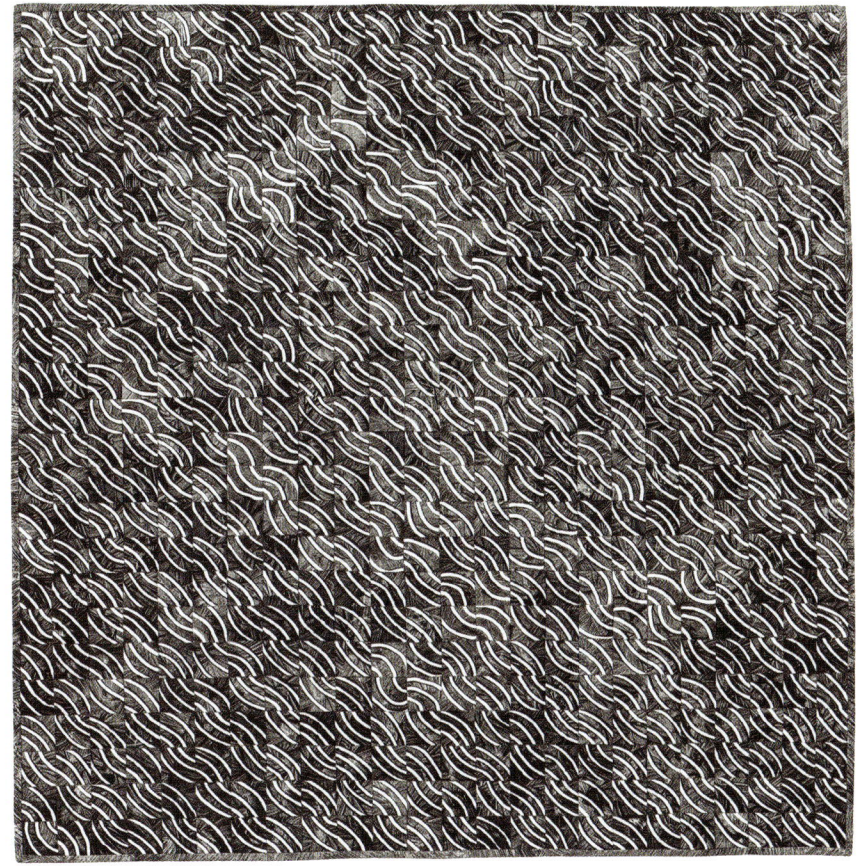

BENEDICTE CANEILL
Larchmont, New York

Whitewater
36" x 36"

**Cotton fabrics, textile paints, Plexiglass plate,
marking tools, polyester batting, polyester thread**

Mono-printed, machine pieced and quilted

*Whitewater arose from my fascination with pattern around me, including
in nature. I have been exploring how the repetition of one form leads to new
possibilities of rhythm. Each square repeats the same motif of three lines
but the hand gesture of drawing each line and square individually
makes for unique variations. How the squares are assembled shows the
possibilities of design and reality; in this case, evoking movement of water.*

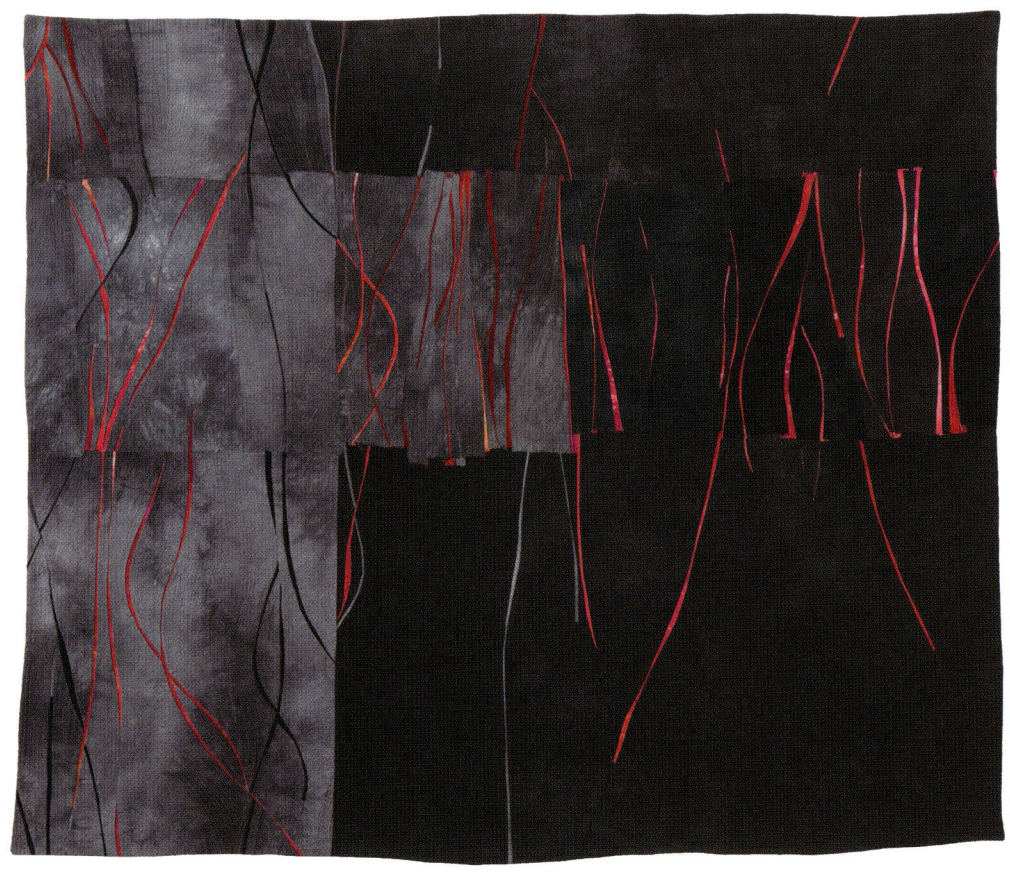

BETH CARNEY
Yonkers, New York

Chasms 23
54″ x 67″

Hand-dyed cotton fabric, silk batting, Madeira PolyNeon threads

Raw-edged fusing, machine pieced and quilted

Chasms 23 is my exploration of how one can use line and color to tell a story. In this piece, the bright colors traveling through the sometimes black, sometimes murky-gray, become a symbol of who we are as we move through experiences in life that continually challenge us. It is possible to face the darkness and emerge brighter and stronger. This is the essence of our spirit, the memories, and the hopes we carry with us.

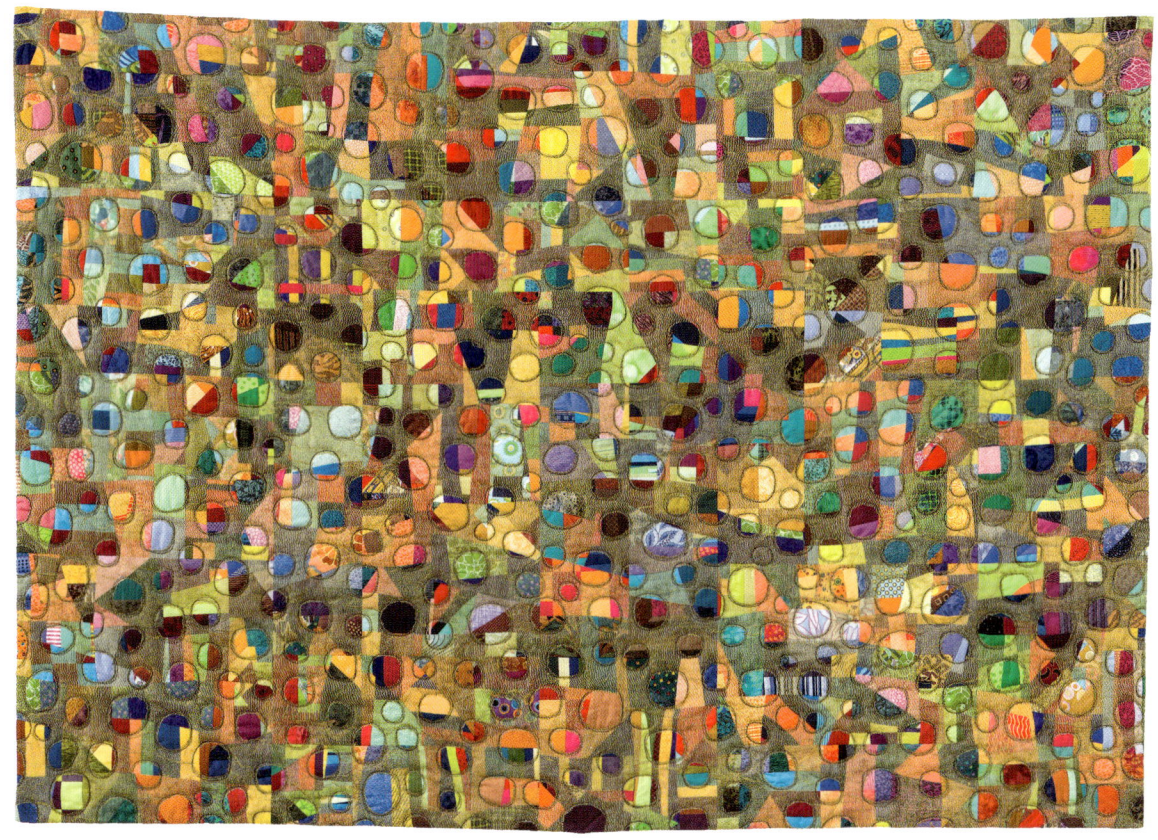

MARYLINE COLLIOUD-ROBERT
Boudry, Neuchâtel, Switzerland

Trous de Mémoire
48″ x 70″

Cotton, cotton mix, synthetic fabric, polyester batting

Reverse appliquéd, machine pieced, and quilted

This piece is about memory and memory gaps. I'm trying to picture thoughts that pop up suddenly in our head, and trying to understand why some do and some remain hidden or lost.

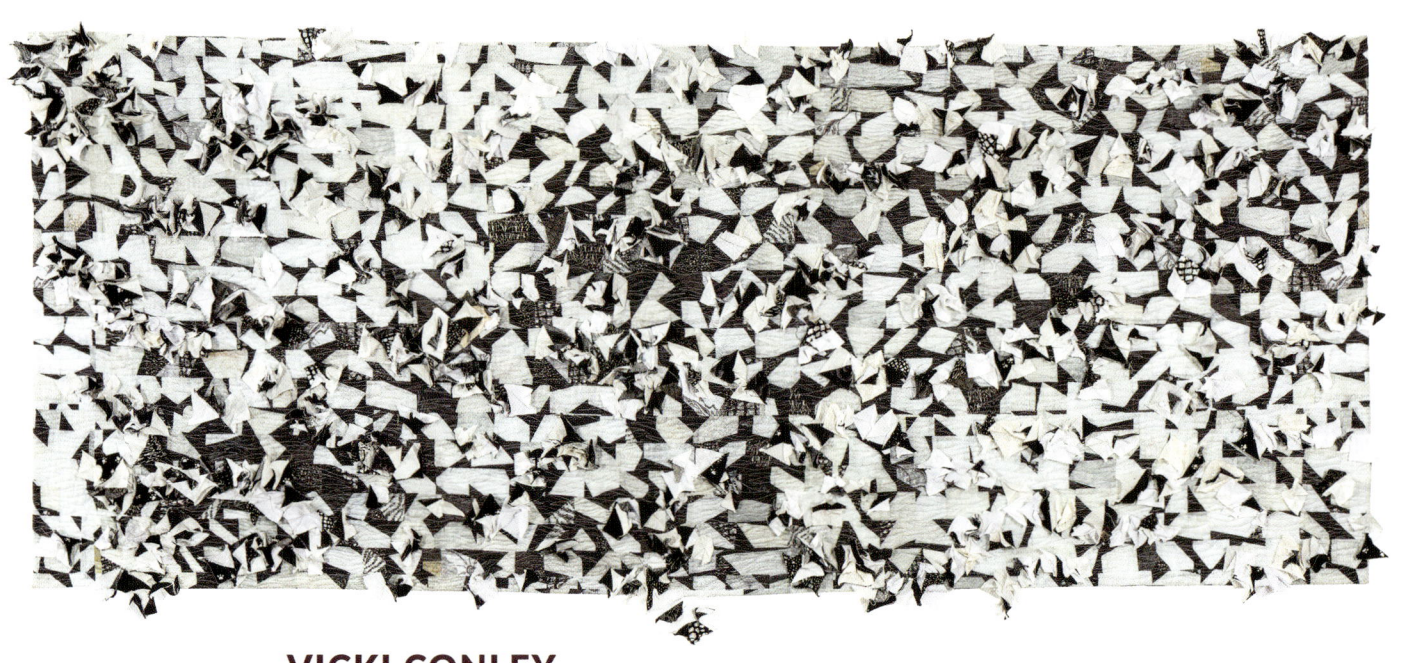

VICKI CONLEY
Ruidoso Downs, New Mexico

Flying Geese
30" x 70"

Commercial cotton, digitally printed cotton sateen, polyester embroidery thread

Machine quilted, machine-pieced 3-D geese, hand stitched

Is it a predator, a change in the wind, a sudden noise, or just a shared internal signal? The spectacle of thousands of snow geese taking to the sky all at once is well worth seeing. The squawking, flapping, and lift off of thousands of birds creates a churning, roiling sky. Yet underneath it all is millennia of instinct, allowing the population to act as one, preventing true turmoil in the face of apparent chaos.

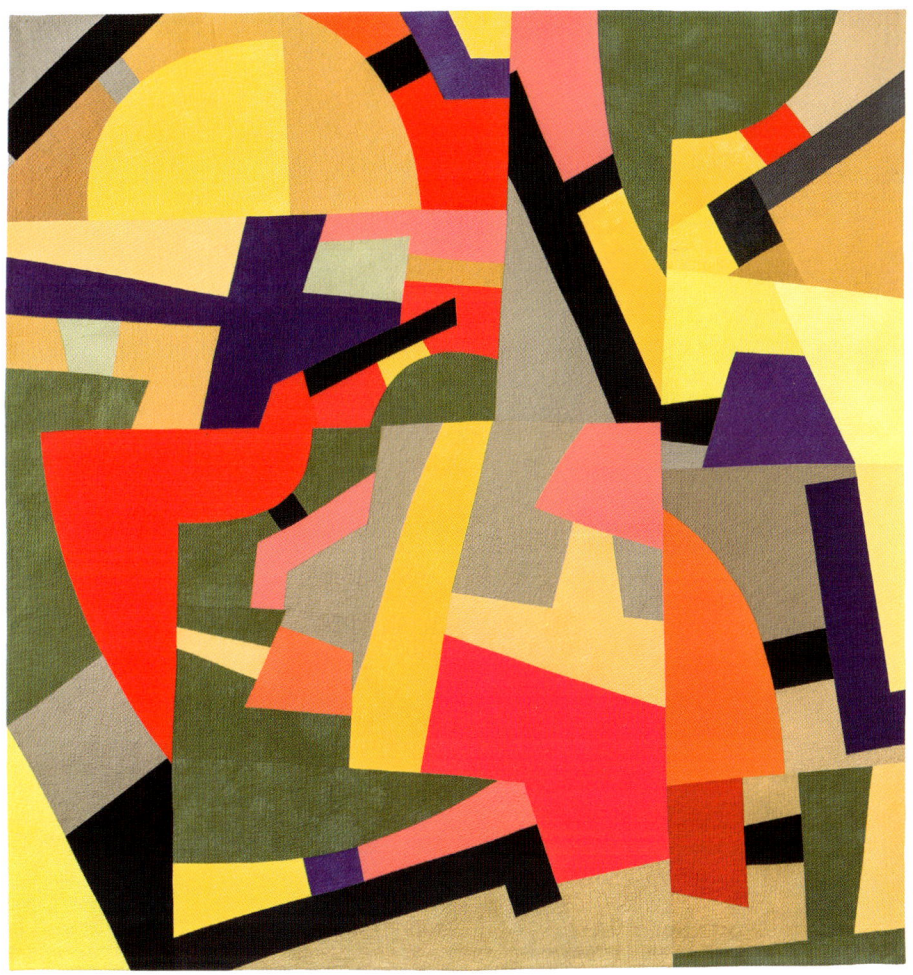

NANCY CORDRY
Seattle, Washington

The Transporter
73″ x 70.5″

Cotton fabric, cotton thread, cotton batting, fabric dye, rotary cutter

Freehand rotary cut, machine pieced, free-motion machine quilted

Riding my bicycle transports me into a sense of freedom and joyfulness and appreciation for the gift of life and good health—away from troubles and worries.

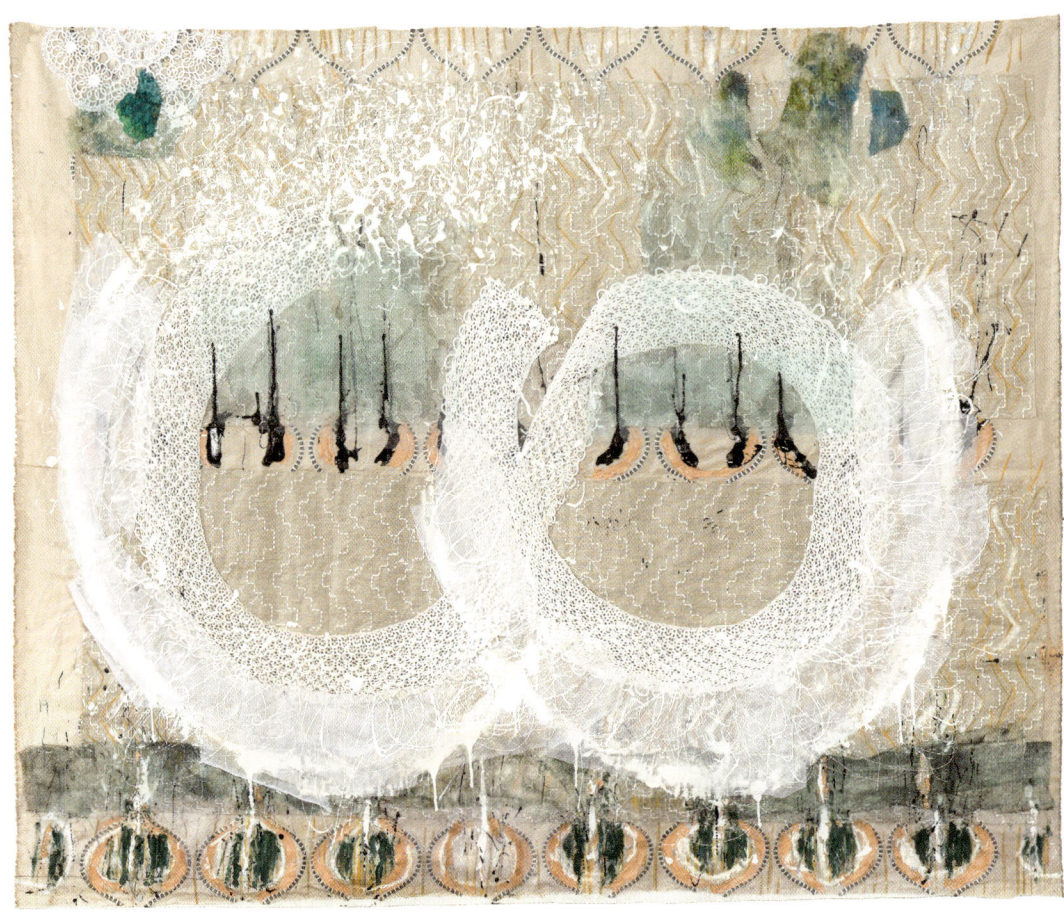

YAEL DAVID-COHEN
London, United Kingdom

Opening
47" x 59"

Old lace, scrim, synthetic curtain, cotton, acrylic paint

Hand painted and sewed

The idea of recycling and reusing of material, giving it a new life, is something I enjoy very much. I enjoy the whole process of hunting for the material (textiles, wire, lace) with the pursuit of an idea of free expression of painting and sewing. The mechanical act of sewing serves as a form of meditation and review of the work from inside in contrast to the spontaneous free expression in painting.

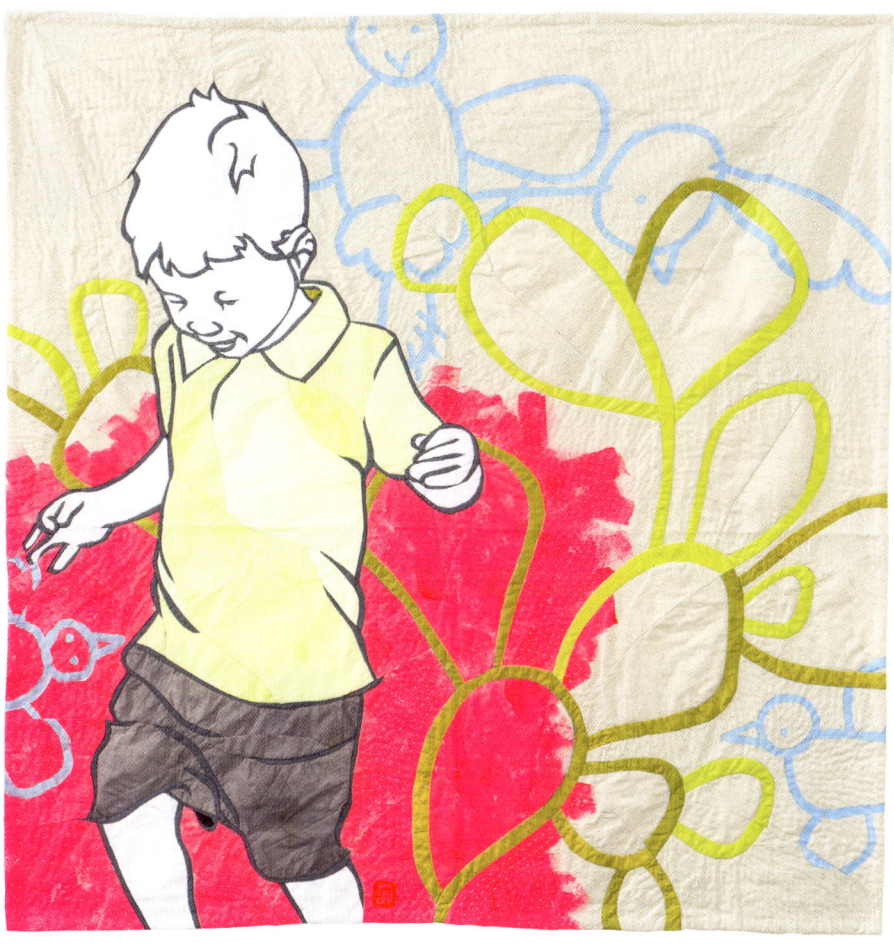

RUTH DE VOS
Mt. Nasura, Washington

This Discovering 1
47" x 47"

Procion fabric dye, Texcraft fabric paint, cotton homespun,
Kona cotton, cotton linen blend, topstitch thread

Hand dyed, hand painted, machine pieced, machine and hand quilted

*There is so much joy to experience in observing a small child discovering
and learning about the world in which he lives. Through the little children,
we who are older are privileged to relive some of their sense of wonder!*

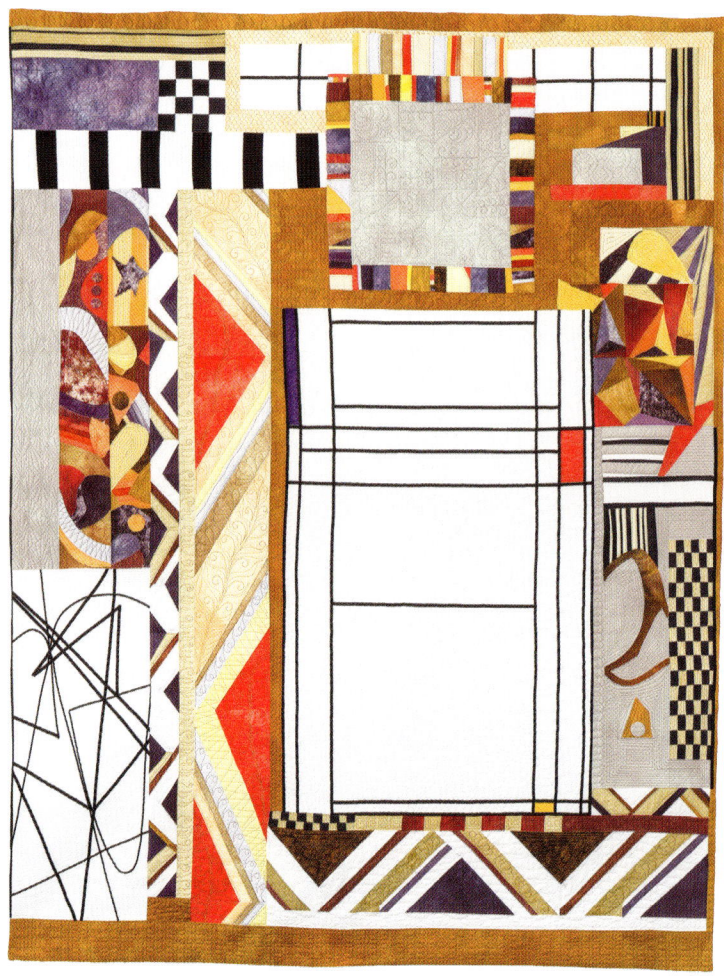

JILL DOSCHER
Skaneateles, New York

Passage
77" x 60"

Artist-dyed and manipulated cotton, grosgrain ribbon, cotton
thread, cotton batting, commercial cotton backing, fabric paint

Machine pieced, hand appliquéd, machine-couched ribbon, machine quilted

*I enjoy a certain "thatness," where my expression and energy is externalized
through color and movement 'that' feel both playful and direct, the sum of all the
parts equaling a magnificent whole. I love the challenge, the process, the shapes,
the fabrics, the textures, the colors, and the surface, and how it develops layer upon
layer, the exploration, the venturing into the unknown and finding the MAGIC.*

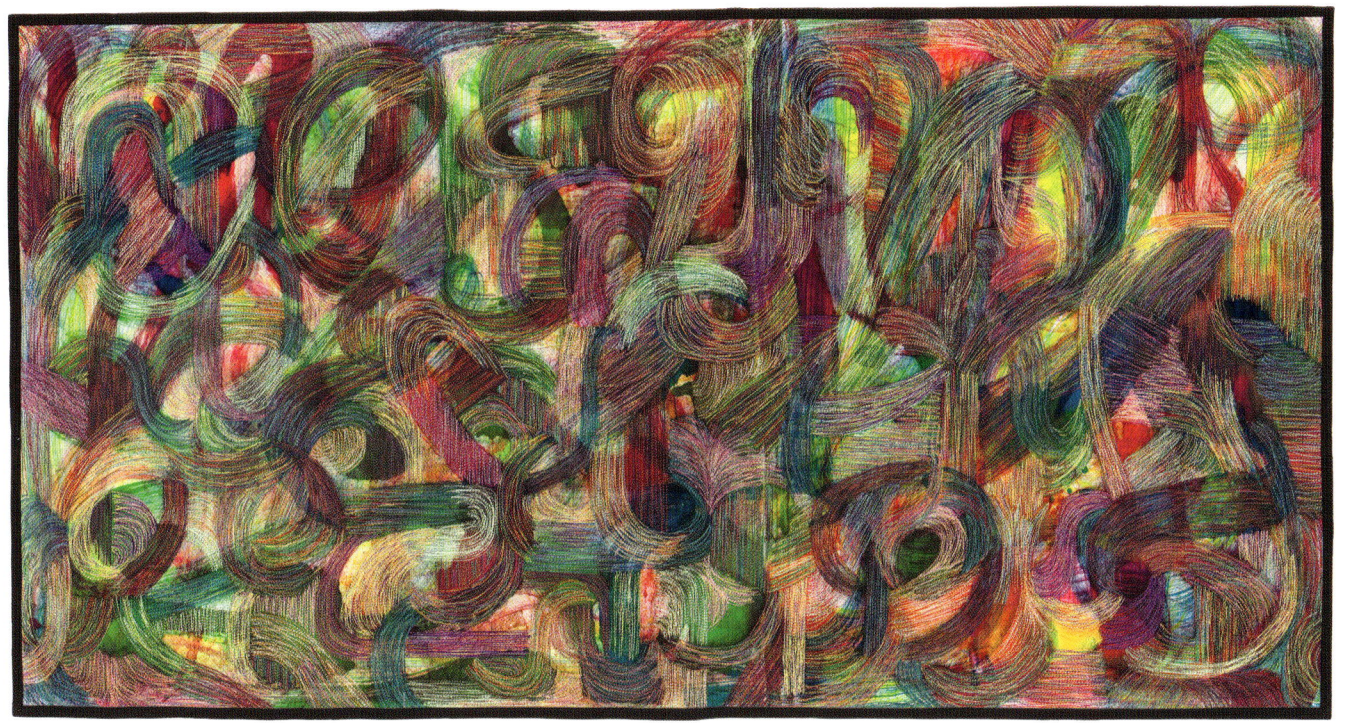

REE FAGAN
Bow, New Hampshire

OBX Seas in April
27" x 52"

Cotton broadcloth fabric, reactive inks,
polyester and cotton thread, wool batting

Threadwork, painted fabric

The Outer Banks (OBX) in North Carolina is a special place, although I could never live there. It takes me five minutes to put on my sneakers—I get so mesmerized by the seas. Just as the seas have a lot of movement, so does this piece. Only variegated threads were used in order to create the organic nature of this work. The foundation fabric was painted in this whole cloth quilt.

PAMELA FITZSIMONS

Mount Vincent,
New South Wales,
Australia

Werekata 4
57" x 26"

Silk, plant dyes
(eucalyptus leaves),
wool batting,
silk thread

Fabrics layered,
hand stitched

*Werekata, the
Kookaburra, calls
his family's territorial
boundaries each
morning and evening
on the property we
share with over 160
different bird species
and many endangered
mammals. 230-year-old
fossils embedded in
the sandstone cliffs
and creek bed of Bow
Wow Gorge have
endured the ravages
of time, but can our birds
and animals survive?*

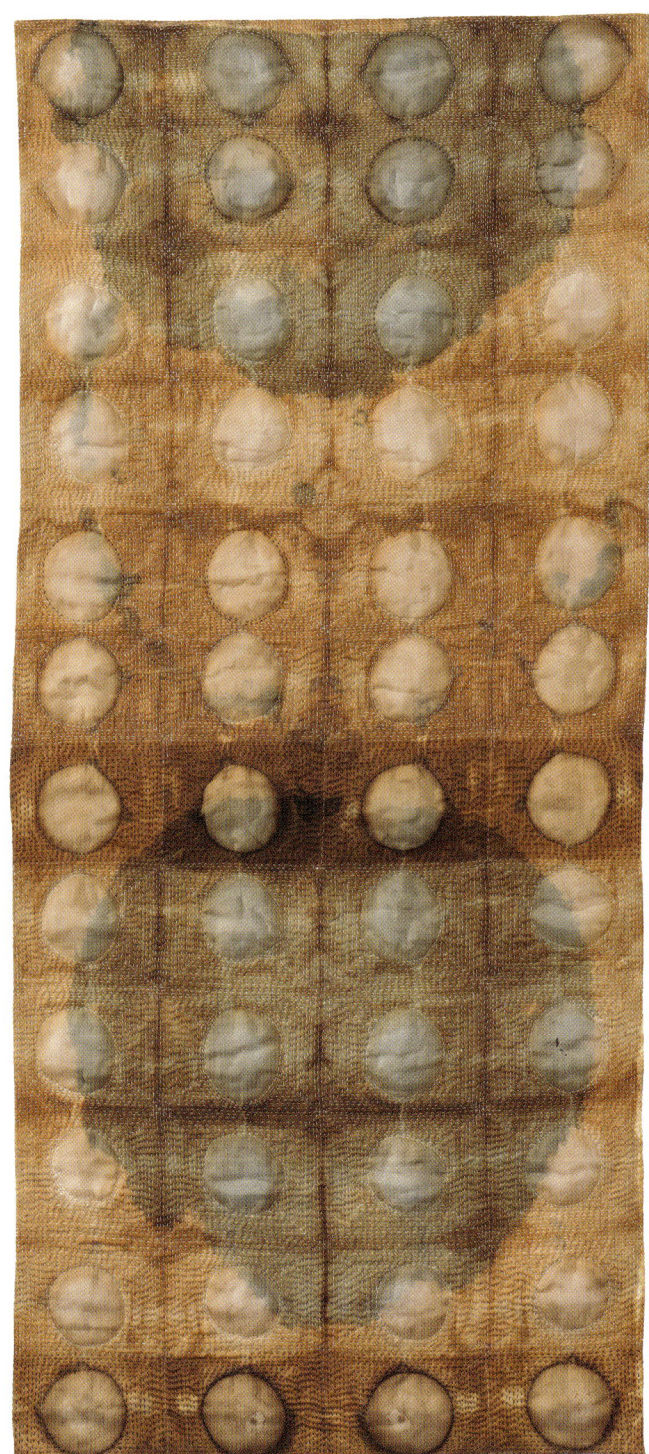

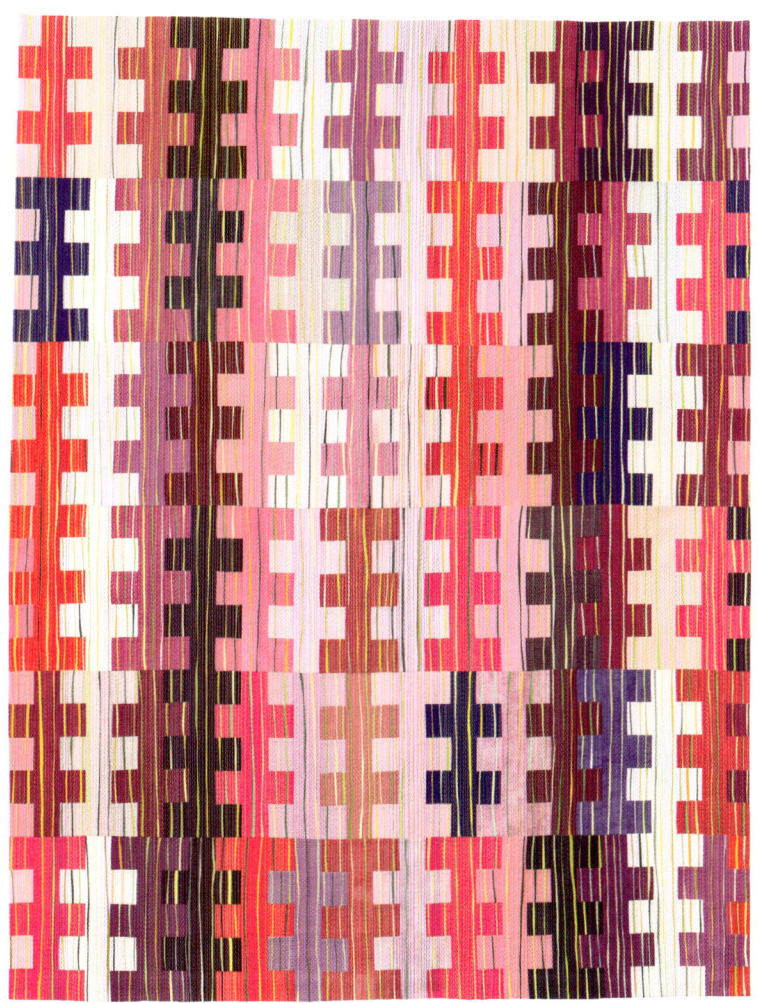

DIANA FOX
Denver, Colorado

Rain Series #2: Purple
57″ x 72″

Hand-dyed and commercial cotton

Machine pieced and quilted

Through the exploration of fiber as my medium, I find mark-making, abstraction, and use of color as constant and endless sources of inspiration. Often my work is stimulated by spirituality and nature, and my artistic process varies from setting out with a plan to complete spontaneity. I am endlessly excited by the creative process.

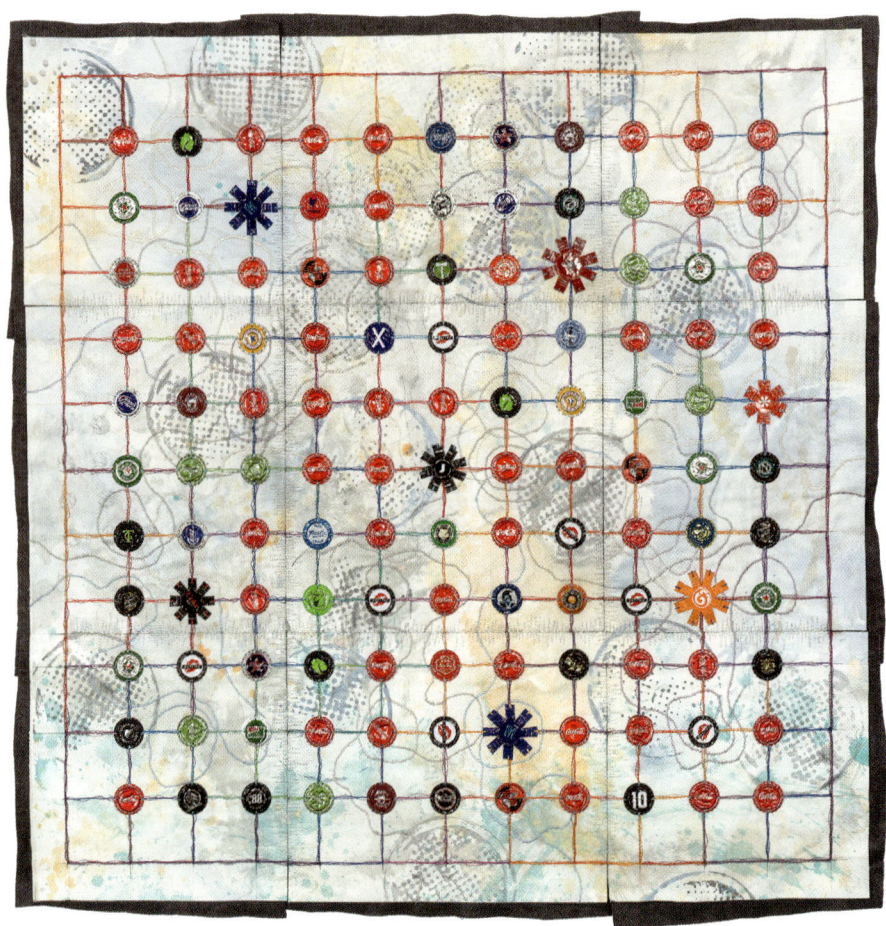

JUDITH QUINN GARNETT
Portland, Oregon

Quilt of Fantastical Things
40" x 40"

Acrylic paint, gesso, cotton canvas, silk, rayon, cotton, and polyester thread, wool/rayon felt, PVA, woven and printed commercial linen, bottle caps

Acrylic painted and stamped canvas, machine appliquéd, embellished with found objects and thread drawing

I find inspiration in ordinary objects and often use them in unexpected ways to express my visual ideas about repetition and pattern. It was natural, then, that circles in a sketch made me think of the bottle caps my son, Jake, has collected all his life. When he saw the small sample where I tested them, he generously gave me his collection to use in a quilt, thus the "J" in the central bottle cap.

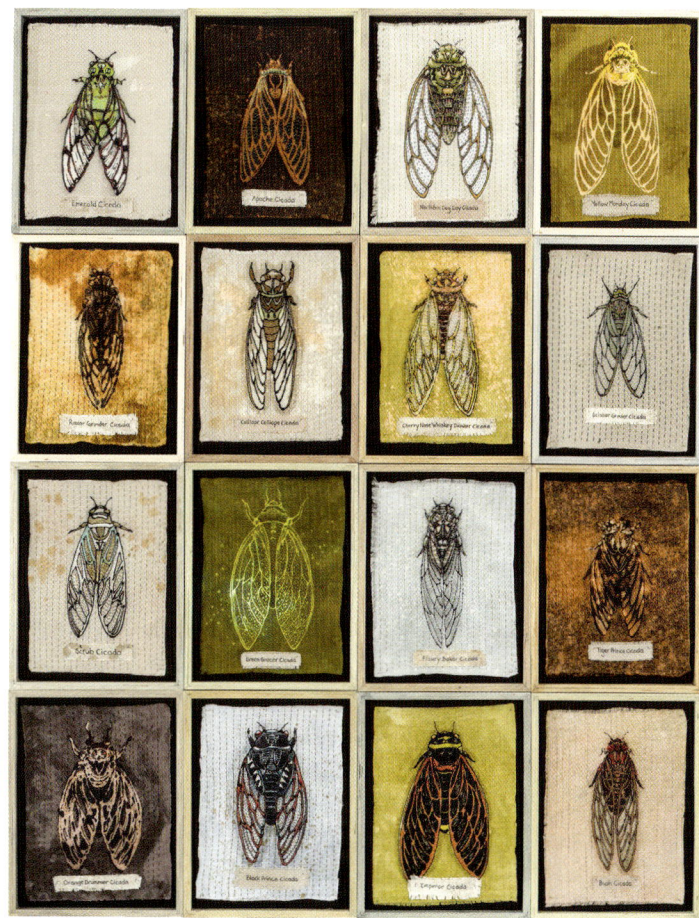

KATE GORMAN
Westerville, Ohio

A Chorus of Cicadas
56″ x 44″

Linen, Procion dyes, industrial felt, embroidery thread, entomology pins, cradled wood panels, plywood, nuts, bolts

Dyed, drawn, and painted with thickened dyes, discharged with thickened bleach, hand stitched, sewn onto industrial felt, mounted in cradled wood panel boxes, mounted on plywood

I've lived in Ohio through several 17-year hatching cycles, and have heard the oscillating buzz, but only recently have I really looked at the visually complex cicada. Its image is drawn on linen, which is both coarse and soft, causing unpredictability even in my most deliberate markings. Stitching suggests the filigree of the creature's exoskeleton and wings. Individual quilts are mounted on wool and pinned in shadowboxes that reference scientific specimen cases.

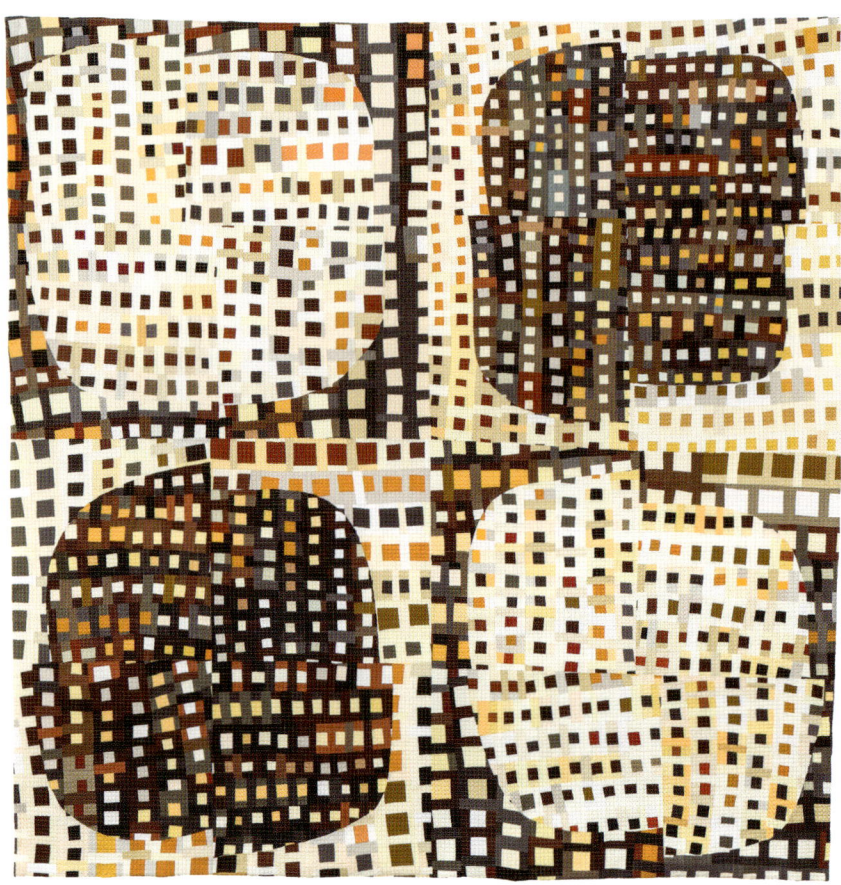

JULIA GRAZIANO
Manlius, New York

Frameworks III
77" x 78"

Commercial cottons, cotton batting, cotton thread

Machine pieced and quilted

In this series of works, I have used this grid technique to study repeating patterns and shape. The energy from this work is derived from all the intricate piecework of thousands of seams and variations in size. The small pieces develop into pleasing abstract shapes. The palette used enhances the graphics expression. The quilted grid overlays the work to reinforce the expression of pattern.

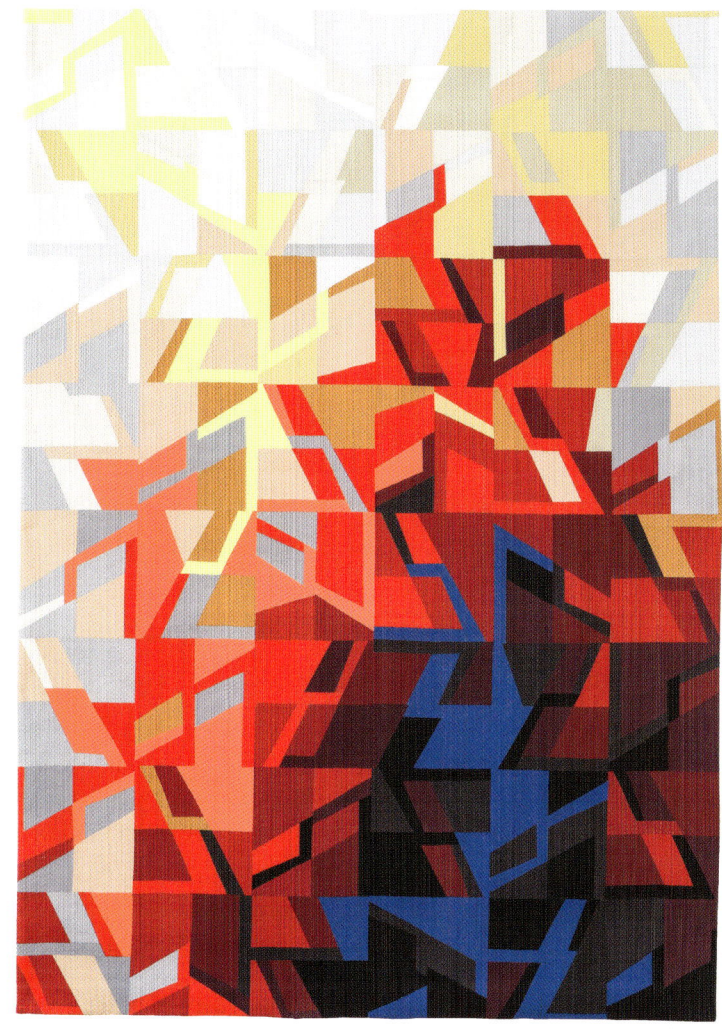

KERRI GREEN
Dallas, Texas

Prometheus
78″ x 56″

Hand-dyed cotton fabric, cotton batting, thread

Machine pieced and quilted

Prometheus is best known in Greek mythology as the deity who stole fire from Mount Olympus and gave it to man, thereby saving mankind from Zeus's wrath. This artwork expresses that fiery moment of delivery. During construction I fell into the comfort of using a self-drafted repetitive pattern, which allowed me to focus solely on color, energy, and movement.

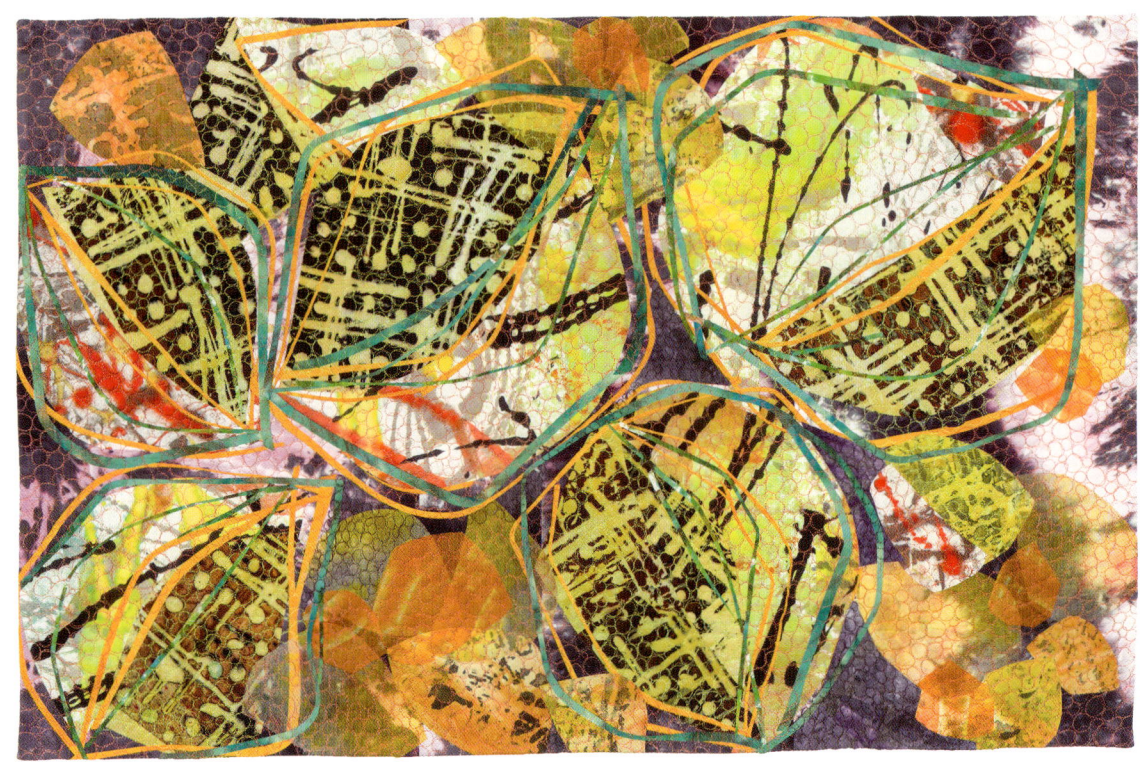

PATTY HAWKINS
Estes Park, Colorado

Jazzed
30.5″ x 48″

Hand-dye-marked cottons and silks, Wonder Under fusible for direct appliqué composition construction, cotton batting, rayon thread

Dye painted, deconstructed abstract silkscreen, low water immersion, fused/direct appliqué construction, machine quilted

Jazzed is my newest abstract expression, always inspired by nature: aspen trees, foliage, or our local rock formations. "Playing" with color and most lyrical "sketch" markings is a desire to add a drawn element, giving the audience a chance to linger.

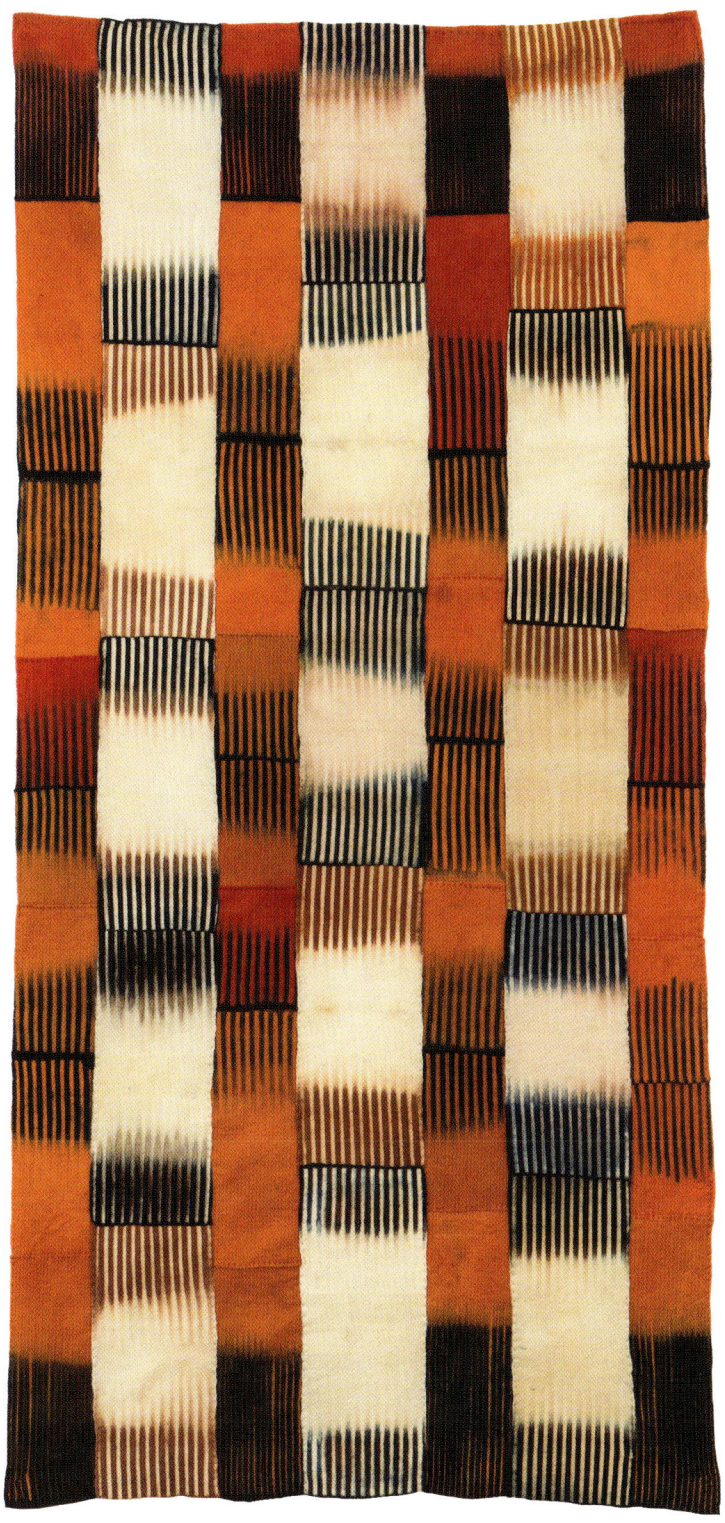

ANA LISA HEDSTROM
La Honda, California

Ladders II
73″ x 38″

Wool felt

Shibori carved
clamp resist madder,
indigo, pomegranate,
and tea dyes,
hand stitched

*I have been fascinated
by the ancient kyokechi
carved clamp resist
textiles in the Shosoin in
Nara, Japan. These silks
have pictorial designs
where a variety of dyes
penetrated different
channels. My adaptation
is very simple—just stripes
cut into the blocks. The
piecing becomes the
most important part
of the graphic design.
I love using natural
dyes for their glowing
quality that enhances
the bold geometry.*

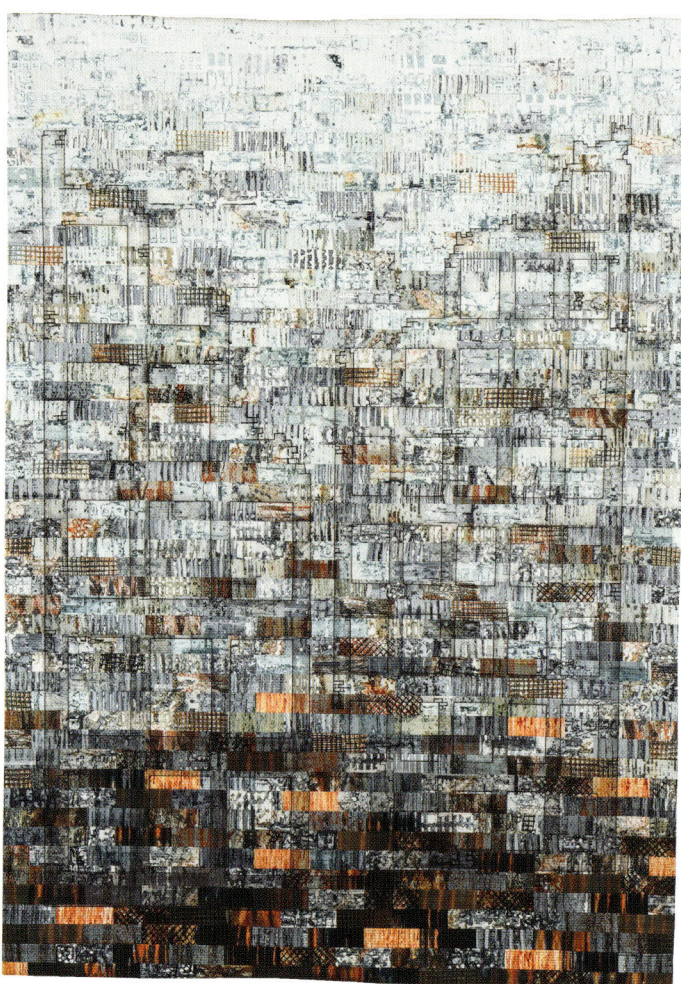

LEAH HIGGINS
Eccles, Manchester, United Kingdom

Ruins 7
98″ x 71″

Hand-dyed and printed cotton fabrics, Procion cold water reactive thickened dyes, acrylic wadding, Madeira cotton threads, Markel oil pastel

Pieced and machine quilted, oil pastel added to finished quilt

Ruins 7 is part of a series that explores what happens to buildings when we stop using them. It references buildings and cities destroyed by war. London, Dresden, Hiroshima, Lebanon, New York. Hate and war destroys lives. It destroys buildings and tears cities apart. Do we rebuild? Or is the thought of burying that hate under new buildings too painful? Should we allow nature to reclaim the buildings, to cover the ground, to soothe the pain?

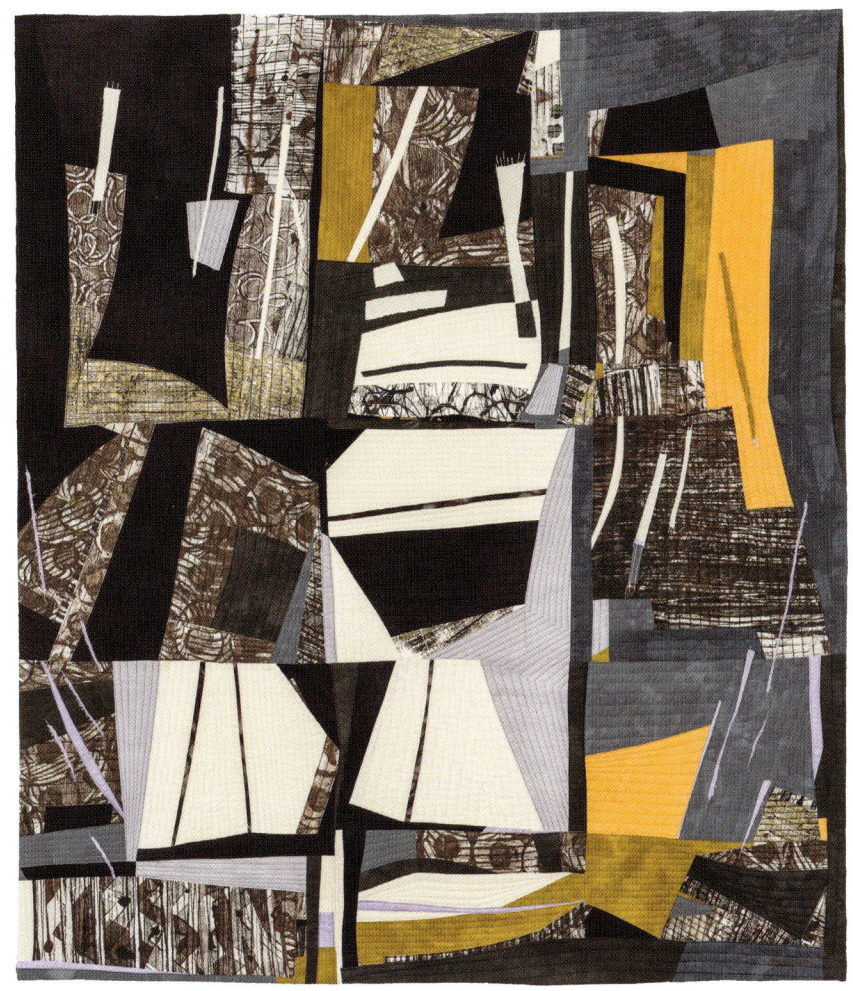

ROSEMARY HOFFENBERG
Wrentham, Massachusetts

Regatta
43″ x 38″

Cotton, thread, natural batting

Dyed, mono-printed, painted, machine pieced,
raw edge appliquéd, machine quilted

*Color, shape, and their overall impact are the driving forces
in my quilts. These elements are what I respond to viscerally;
thus, they generate the process of my quilt design.*

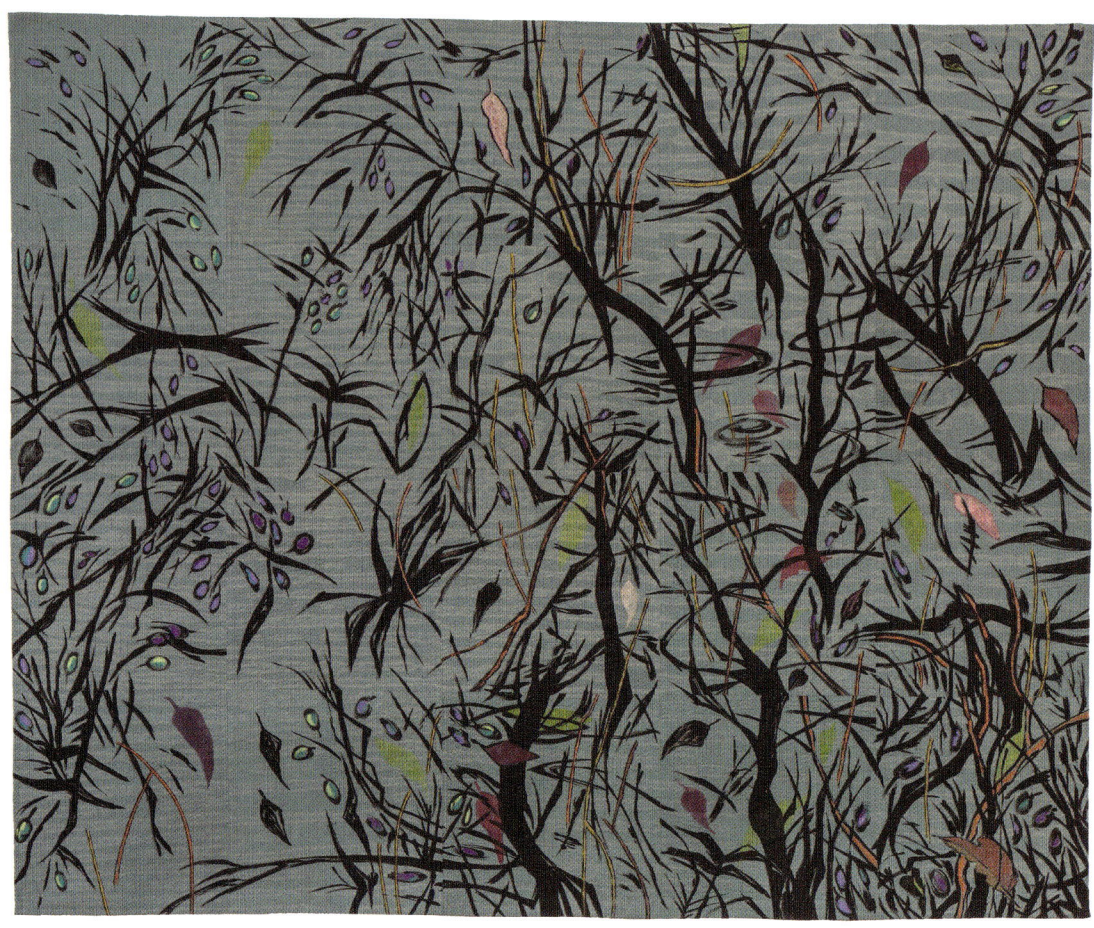

JUDY HOOWORTH
Morisset, New South Wales, Australia

Creek Drawing #15
50.5″ x 62.5″

Cotton, acrylic paint and ink, water-soluble crayons,
textile medium, cotton polyester batting, cotton thread

Discharged with bleach gel, hand drawn and painted, machine pieced and quilted

My quilt is about place, particularly Dora Creek, which flows near my home. Walking along the creek is part of my routine, integral to my life and artistic practice. I document each walk with photographs and drawings. I'm interested in patterns: light on water, trees and branches, grasses and leaves; and the changing colors and moods created by variations in the weather day by day.

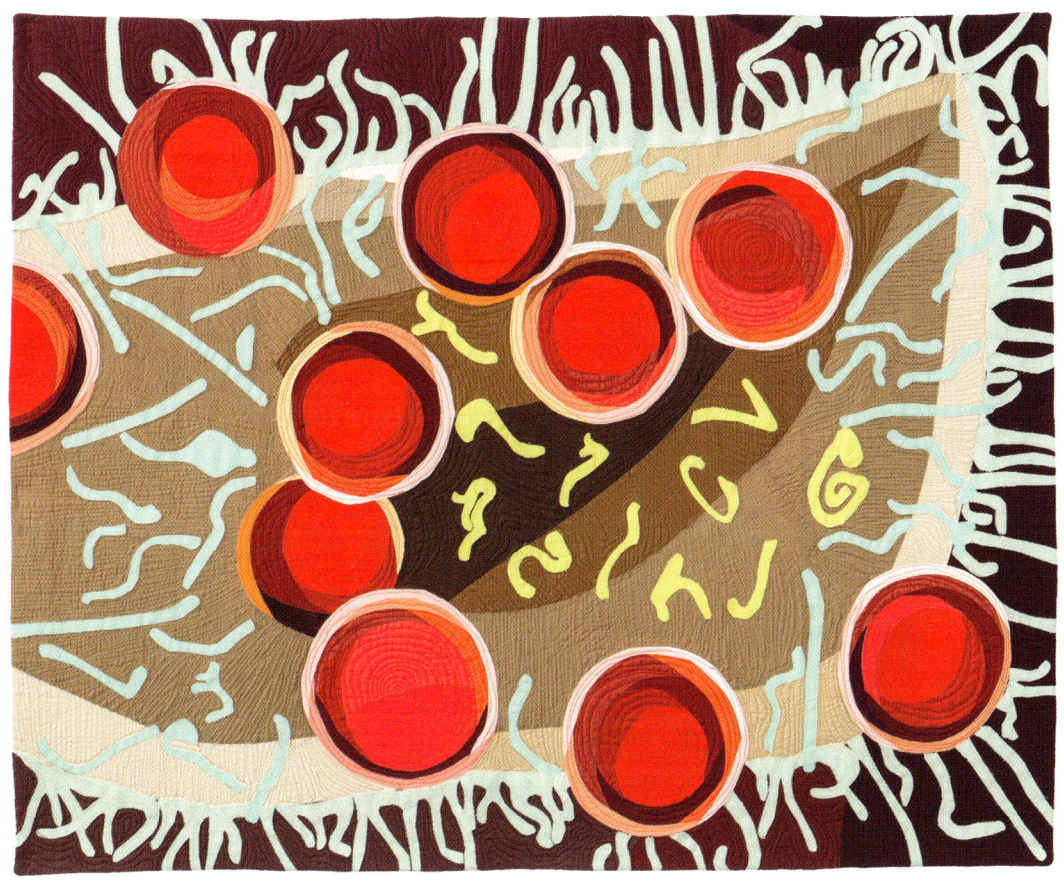

JEAN HOWARD
Auxvasse, Missouri

Cellular Level I: T-cells Attacking
a Breast Cancer Cell
49.5″ x 39″

Cotton fabric, cotton thread, cotton batting

Raw edge appliquéd, machine pieced and quilted

I have studied and worked in the healthcare field for decades, and likewise have sewed and quilted for decades. Cellular Level I: T-cells Attacking a Breast Cancer Cell is a melding of my love of science, awe of the microscopic universe, and love for using fabric as an art medium. In this piece, I have taken something considered microscopic and ugly, and translated it into an over-sized celebration of color.

SARA IMPEY
Colchester, Essex,
England

The Deconstructed Quilt
71" x 46"

Calico, felt and pelmet vilene batting, polyester threads

Free-motion machine stitched text, machine pieced and quilted

This quilt is a comment on the tension between creative practice and academia. The viewer is invited to analyze the quilt via a series of increasingly absurd and laborious instructions until what is left is quite literally a "deconstructed" quilt—functionally useless and with the areas that normally carry the content missing.

TO DECONSTRUCT THE QUILT, FOLLOW THIS STEP-BY-STEP GUIDE. 1) CONSULT A VARIETY OF DICTIONARIES AND COMPARE THEIR DEFINITIONS OF A QUILT. STUDY ITS ETYMOLOGY — LATIN 'CULCITA', A SACK FILLED WITH FEATHERS, A MATTRESS. MAKE NOTES. 2) RESEARCH INTO THE ORIGINS OF PATCHWORK AND QUILTING. INVESTIGATE THE THEORY THAT THEY FIRST EVOLVED AS ECONOMY MEASURES. EXAMINE ANTIQUE TEXTILES FOR EXAMPLES OF PATCHWORK AND QUILTING. WRITE AN ESSAY. 3) EXPLORE THE DEVELOPMENT OF BOTH DECORATIVE AND FUNCTIONAL QUILTMAKING IN THE 18th AND 19th CENTURIES. ASSESS THE CULTURAL SIGNIFICANCE OF THE QUILT DURING THIS PERIOD AND DISCUSS ITS ROLE AS A GIFT, A FAMILY HEIRLOOM, A RITE OF PASSAGE OR A COMMUNAL ACTIVITY. DESCRIBE HOW DESIGNS AND TECHNIQUES VARIED FROM PLACE TO PLACE. SEARCH FOR IMAGES OF QUILTS TO ILLUSTRATE THESE POINTS IN OLD BOOKS AND MAGAZINES. TRACE THE HISTORY OF PATTERN NAMES ASSOCIATED WITH TRADITIONAL PATCHWORK, SUCH AS LOG CABIN AND FLYING GEESE. WRITE A THESIS. 4) TRACK THE FLUCTUATING POPULARITY OF QUILTING IN THE 20th CENTURY AND ANALYSE THE REASONS BEHIND THE 'QUILT REVIVAL' OF THE 1970s. CONDUCT A SOCIOLOGICAL SURVEY INTO THE LIVES OF SELF-IDENTIFIED QUILTERS. ESTIMATE THE VALUE THEY ATTACH TO QUILTMAKING AS A SOURCE OF CREATIVE FULFILMENT, OF A SENSE OF PURPOSE AND OF STATUS WITHIN A GROUP. REPORT ON THE CONTRIBUTION OF NATIONAL QUILT EXHIBITIONS, FABRIC MANUFACTURERS AND PUBLICATIONS TO THE GLOBAL RESURGENCE OF INTEREST IN QUILTING OVER RECENT DECADES. COLLECT RELEVANT DATA AND PRODUCE GRAPHS AND PIE-CHARTS. WRITE A DISSERTATION. 5) COMPILE A LIST OF 21st CENTURY ARTISTS WHO EXPRESS THEMSELVES THROUGH THE MEDIUM OF QUILTMAKING. QUESTION WHY THEY CHOOSE THE QUILT ABOVE OTHER ART FORMS AS A VEHICLE TO CONVEY SOCIAL, POLITICAL OR PERSONAL THEMES. GO TO AS MANY EXHIBITIONS AS POSSIBLE AND TAKE PHOTOGRAPHS (IF ALLOWED). VISIT WEBSITES. ENGAGE IN A DIALOGUE WITH SELECTED ARTISTS VIA EMAIL OR SOCIAL MEDIA. COMPLETE A PhD. 6) SEEK OUT REFERENCES TO PATCHWORK AND QUILTING IN WORKS OF LITERATURE. CONSIDER WHETHER THE WRITERS CHALLENGE OR REINFORCE PRECONCEPTIONS ABOUT QUILTMAKING AND WHETHER THEY USE THE QUILT AS A BACKGROUND DETAIL, AN AID TO CHARACTERISATION OR A PLOT DEVICE. FIND INSTANCES WHERE THE NOTION OF THE QUILT IS EMPLOYED AS A METAPHOR IN THE INTERPRETATION OF LITERARY TEXTS BY SCHOLARS AND CRITICS. GIVE REFERENCES AND PRODUCE A BIBLIOGRAPHY. WRITE A BOOK. 7) DEBATE WHETHER QUILTING IS AN ART OR A CRAFT. FIND QUILTS TO ILLUSTRATE BOTH SIDES OF THE ARGUMENT. CURATE AN EXHIBITION. 8) THE THEORETICAL PART OF THE PROCESS IS NOW COMPLETE. PROCEED TO THE PRACTICAL STAGE. TAKE A QUILT. CAREFULLY UNPICK ALL THE STITCHES. THE QUILT IS NOW SUCCESSFULLY DECONSTRUCTED.

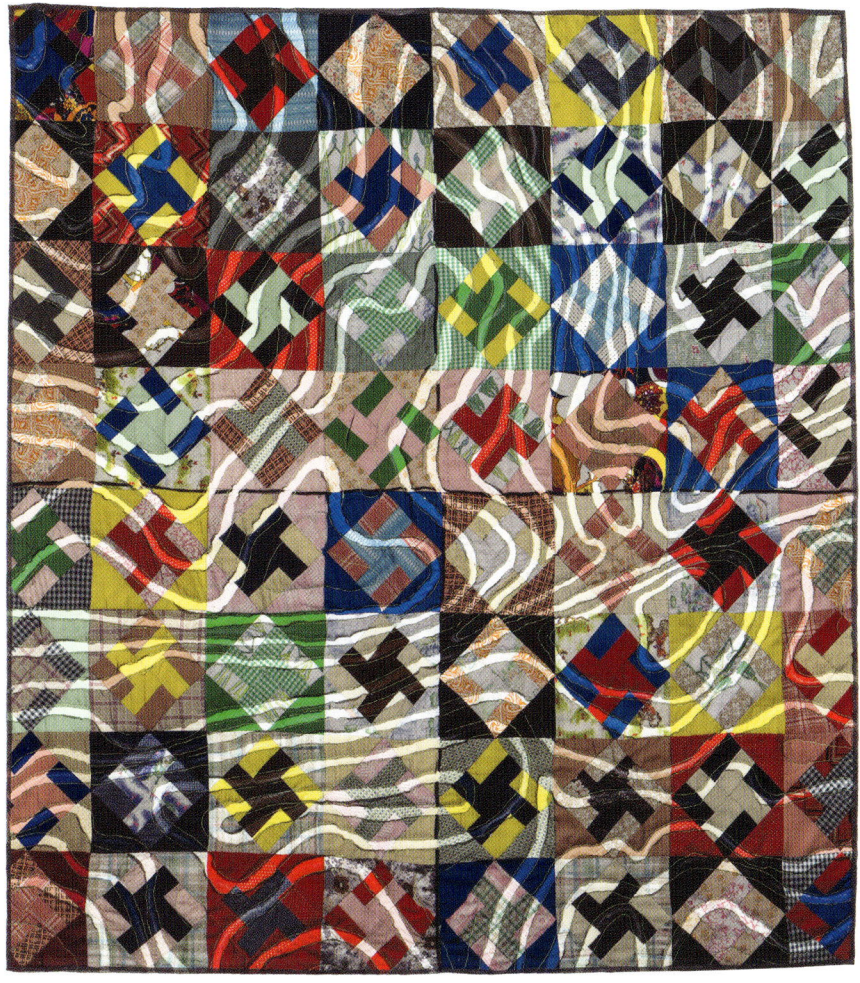

JESS JONES
Decatur, Georgia

Topoquilt Avondale Marta Station
80″ x 73″

Found quilt top, hand-dyed silk organza, cotton batting, thread

Hand-dyed silk, machine quilted, torn appliqué

Quilts often reveal their makers. These found quilt tops inspire me to consider those with whom I share the city landscape. I layer these pieces with geographic data and my own quilting, creating a stitched drawing of the topography of a specific location. I address fellow quilters by connecting formal elements of their work with geographic locations. These playful combinations are more accessible to quilters emphasizing our shared locations and experiences.

BARBARA T. KAEMPFER
Mettmenstetten, Switzerland

Salobre Este
65″ x 40″

Hand-dyed cotton

Pieced, machine quilted

My compositions are created on the design wall. I cut strips and shapes, arrange them on the wall, rearrange, change, until the result pleases me. I love to sew the shapes together and see the piece growing. To me the last step of the process, the quilting, is very important. I love free-motion quilting while listening to good music; for me this is like dancing, as the music adds a certain rhythm.

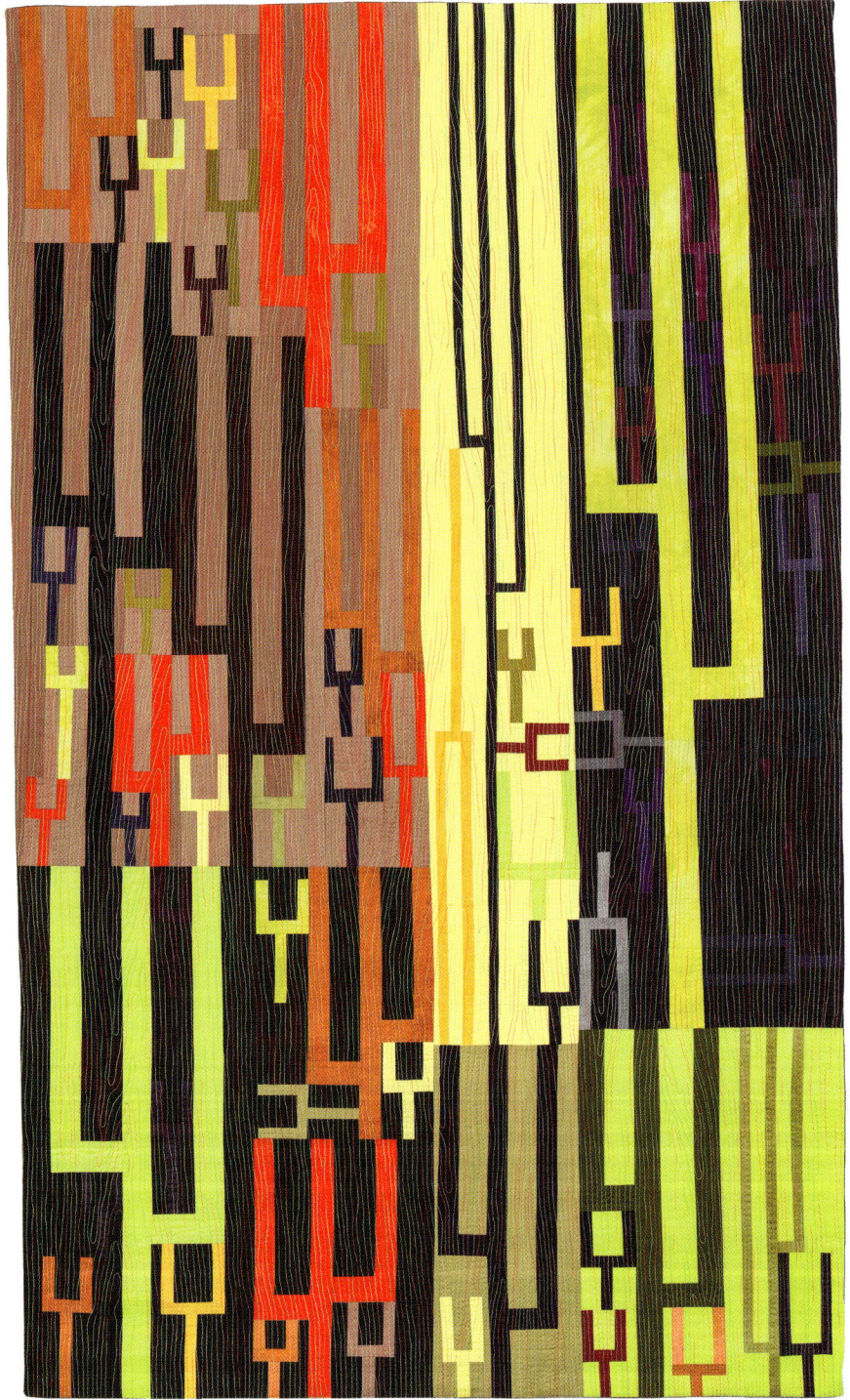

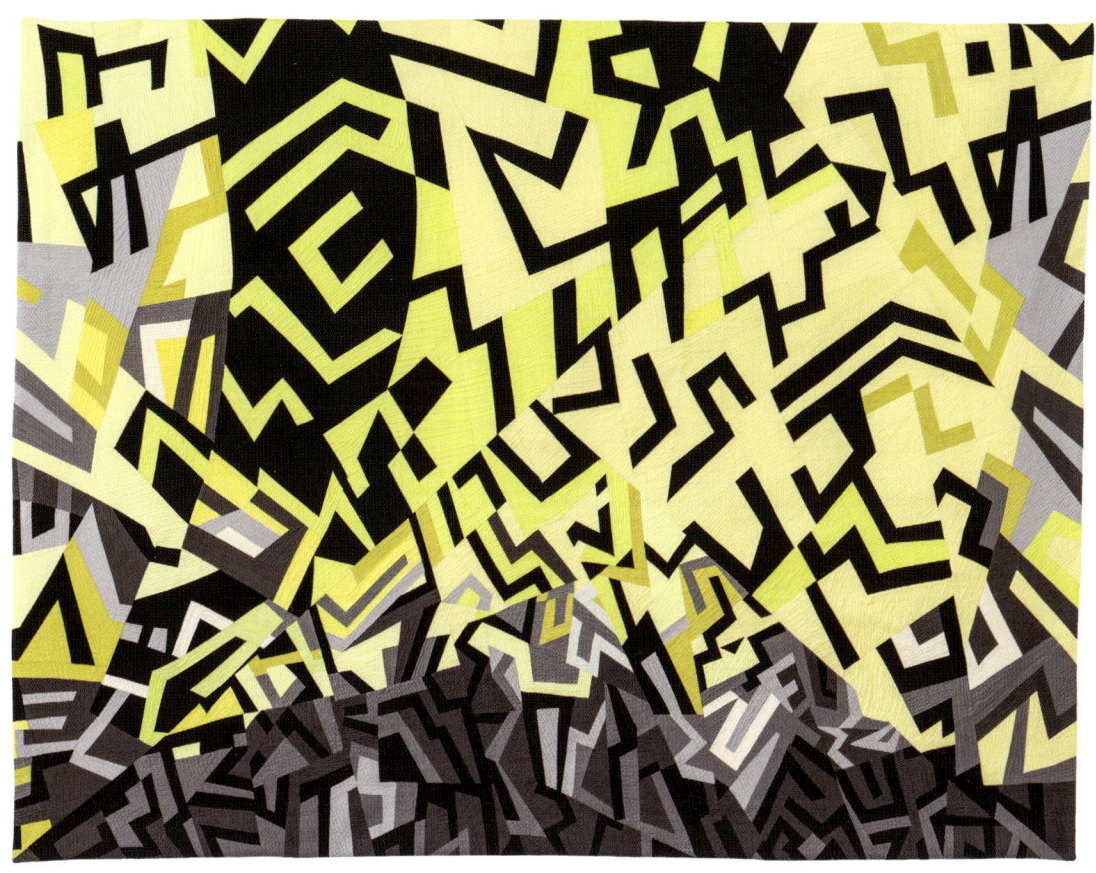

BARBARA KANAYA
Renton, Washington

Chaos of Thoughts
63.5″ x 82″

Commercially dyed cotton

Machine pieced and quilted

My mind is full of thoughts—things to be done, aspirations, fears, loves, hates. The list goes on and on, jumbled up without priority, clogging my head. This is represented by the dark gray at the bottom of the quilt. As the day goes on, I gain clarity! Priorities are set, the day begins as shown by the black and yellow/green. I know my way!

JUDY KIRPICH
Takoma Park, Maryland

Anxiety No. 10/ Retirement
69″ x 42.5″

Cotton fabric hand dyed
by Annette Wink

Machine pieced
and quilted

*Anxiety No. 10 tries
to capture the excitement,
anticipation, and fear
that I felt transitioning
from being a business owner
to a full-time artist as I
approached retirement.*

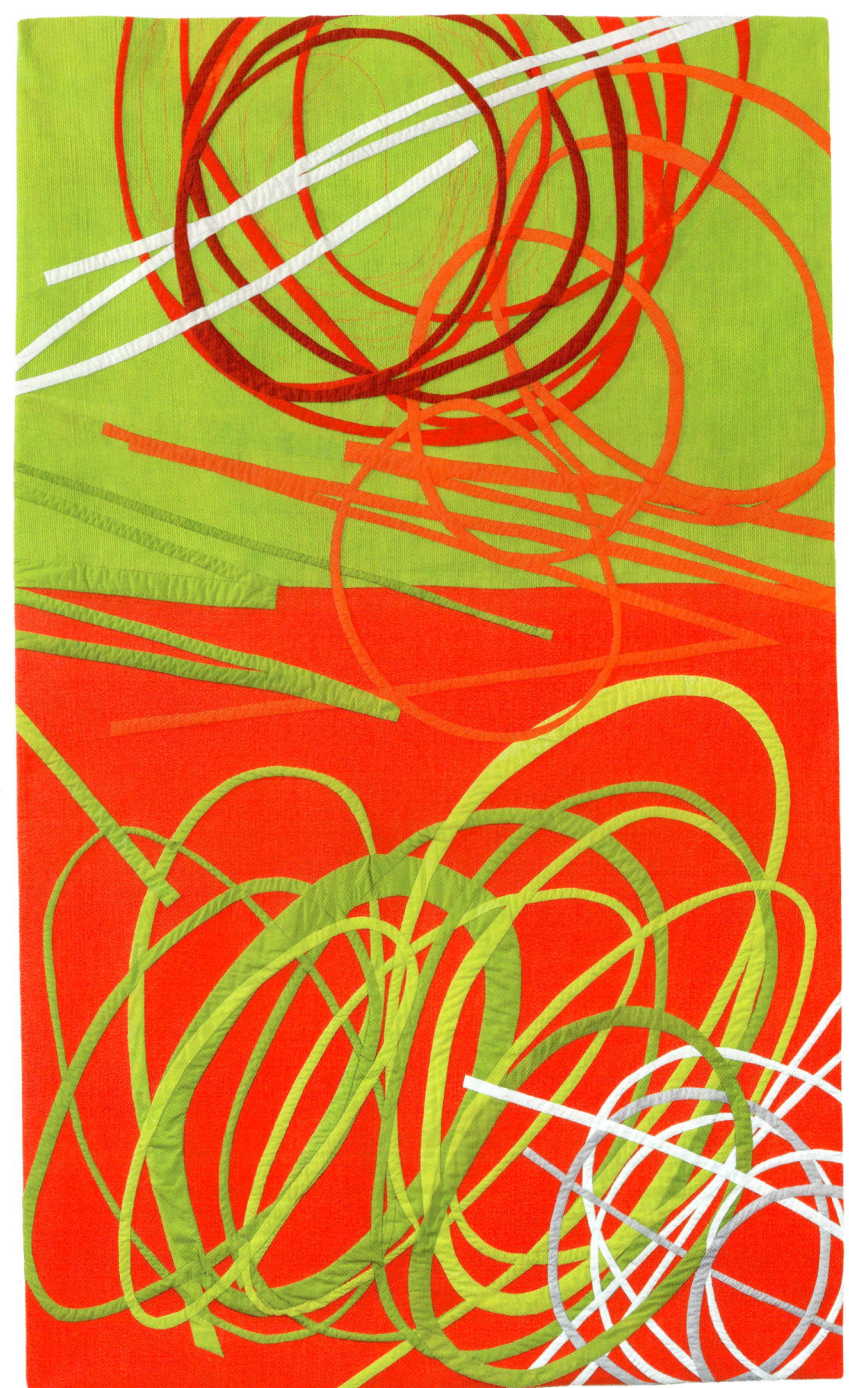

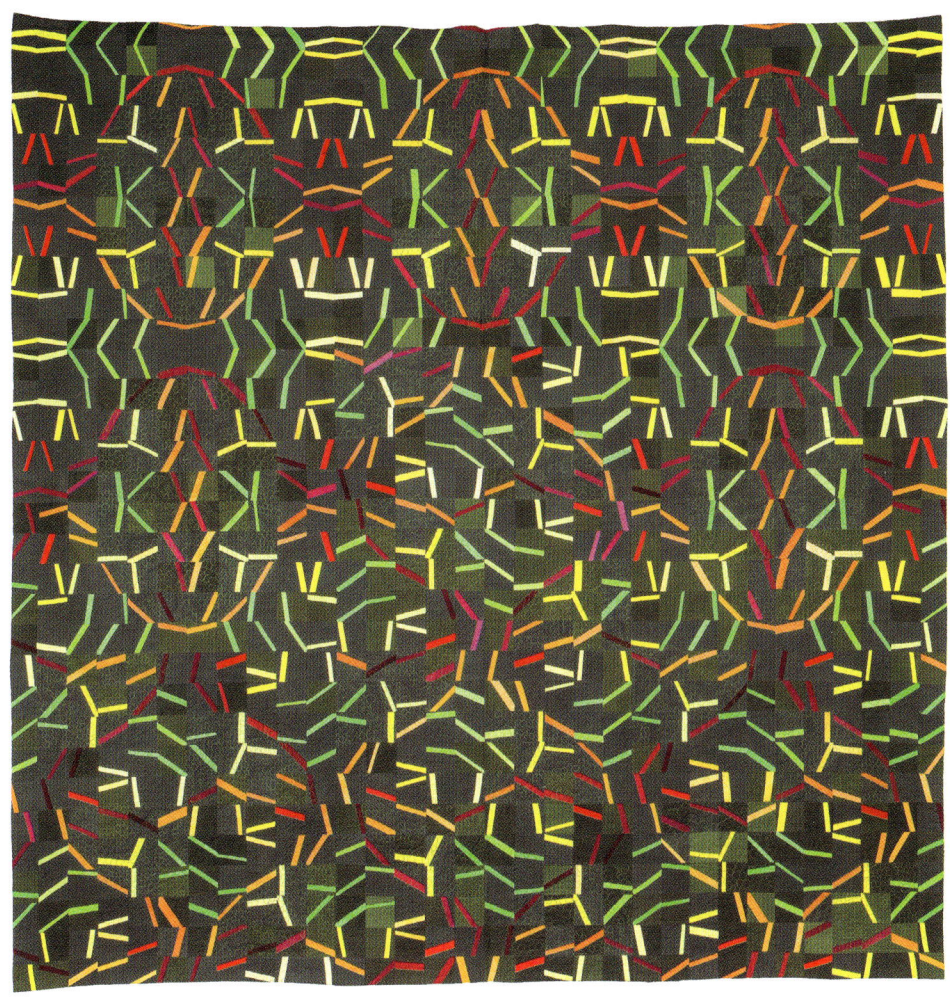

ELKE KLEIN
Beckingen, Germany

Tiles #9: Resolution of the Structure
96″ x 95.5″

Hand-dyed cotton

Machine pieced and quilted

*For me, creating art quilts is a passion. I'm inspired by the interplay of fabric
and color. I love the challenge of envisioning a new design and developing
a detailed plan to bring that vision to life. Working with fabrics and colors
gives me a deep sense of joy, a joy that I am able to pass on to my family.*

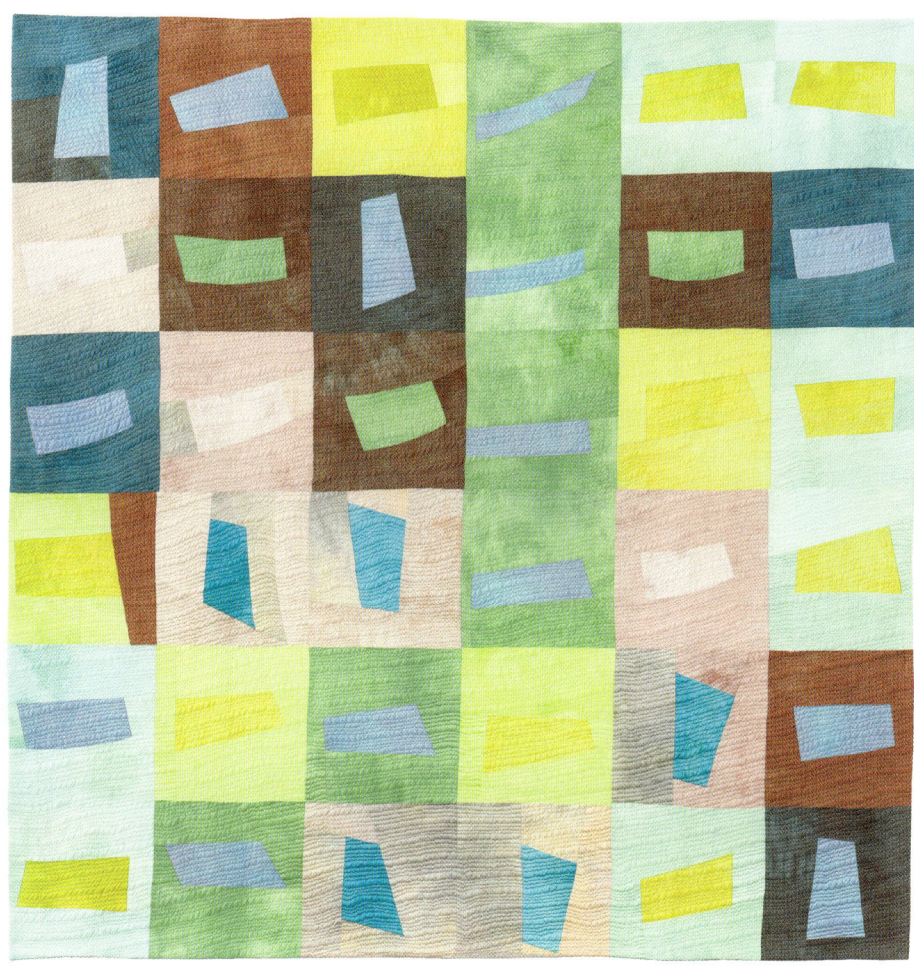

URSULA KOENIG
Bern, Switzerland

Timbres de Mahler
54" x 54"

Hand-dyed cotton fabrics by Heide Stoll-Weber, Heidi Hunninghaus, and Ursula Koenig

Machine pieced and quilted

During the creation of this quilt I was listening to Symphony No. 1 and Symphony No. 7 by Gustav Mahler. Mahler's music is sometimes very harmonious and sometimes it changes into unexpected sounds and rhythm. A kind I want to express with the chosen shades of colors, the forms, and the rhythm.

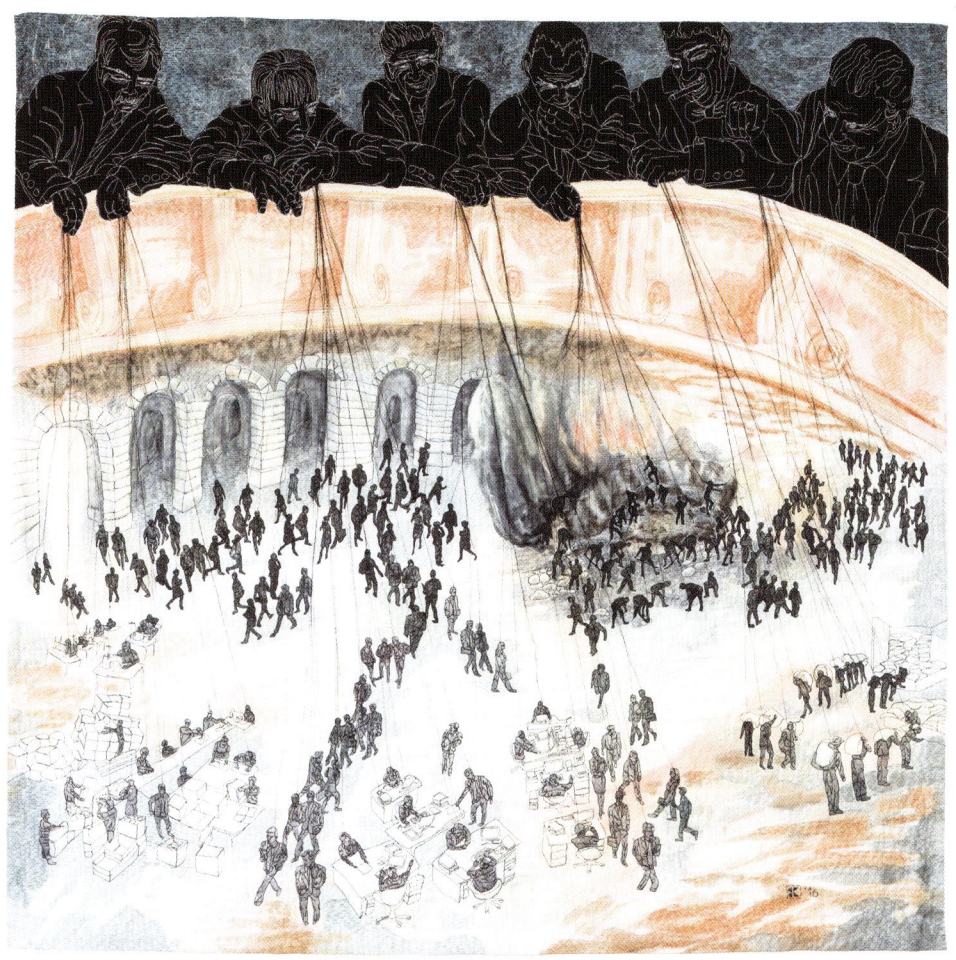

BRIGITTE KOPP
Kasel-Golzig, Germany

Global Players
59″ x 58″

Cotton hand painted by the artist with acrylic inks, painted spun bond, cotton threads

Painted whole cloth, appliquéd, hand and machine quilted

Aren't there a few Global Players holding the reins today? They play not only with goods and raw materials but also with people working for them.

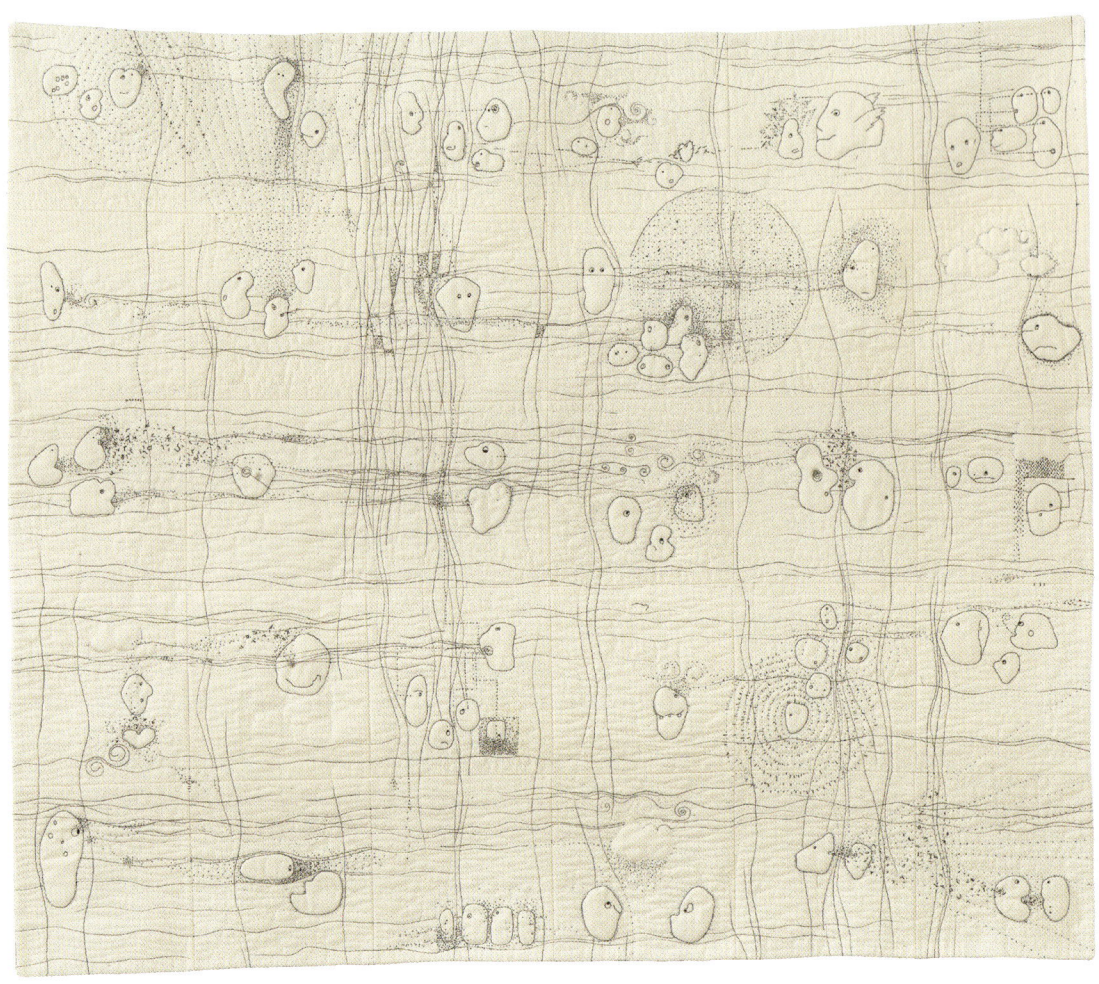

PAULA KOVARIK
Memphis, Tennessee

Secret Life of Stones
40.5″ x 48″

Cotton canvas, wool batting, bamboo batting, cotton fabric, cotton thread

Hand and free-motion machine stitched

The inanimate can become animated when contemplated in silence. There are endless stories to tell. Rock faces, silent personalities, give witness to human folly.

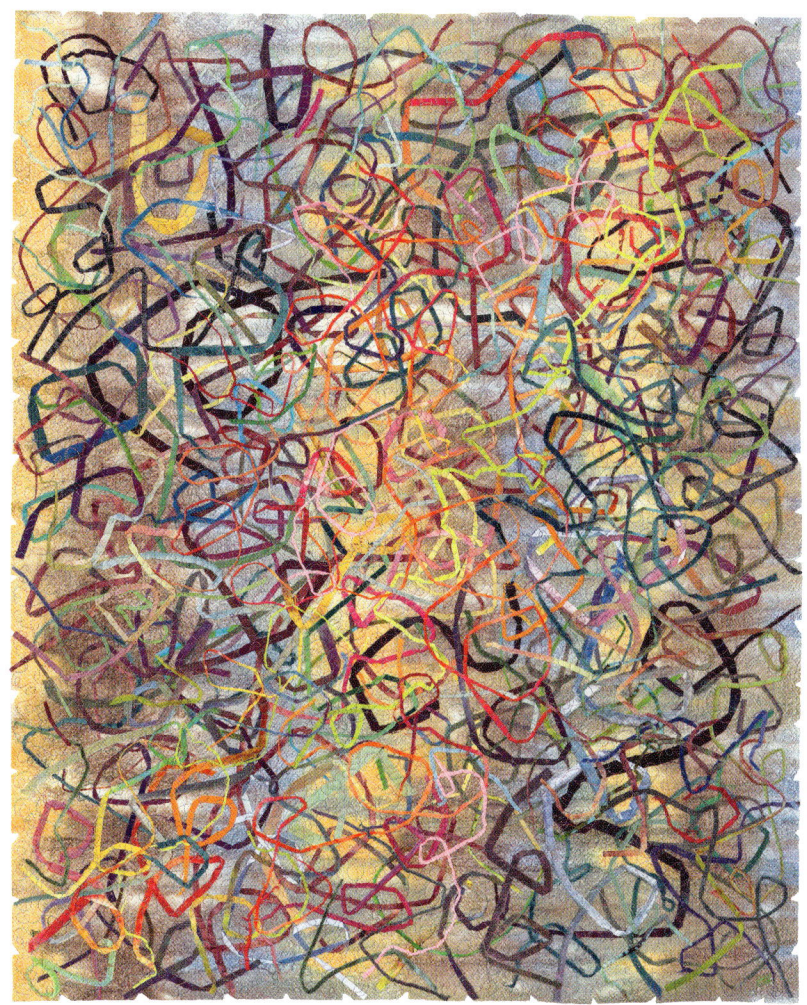

PAT KROTH
Verona, Wisconsin

Full Spin
40″ x 33″

Hand dyed cotton, commercial cotton fabric,
fusible fleece batting, polyester tri-lobal threads

Heat-bonded appliquéd, hand dyed,
improvisational composition, machine stitched

*Cycling…spinning…feeling the breeze as the colors fly by is a favorite activity
of mine. While I'm out on my bike, inspiration wafts in with the wind.*

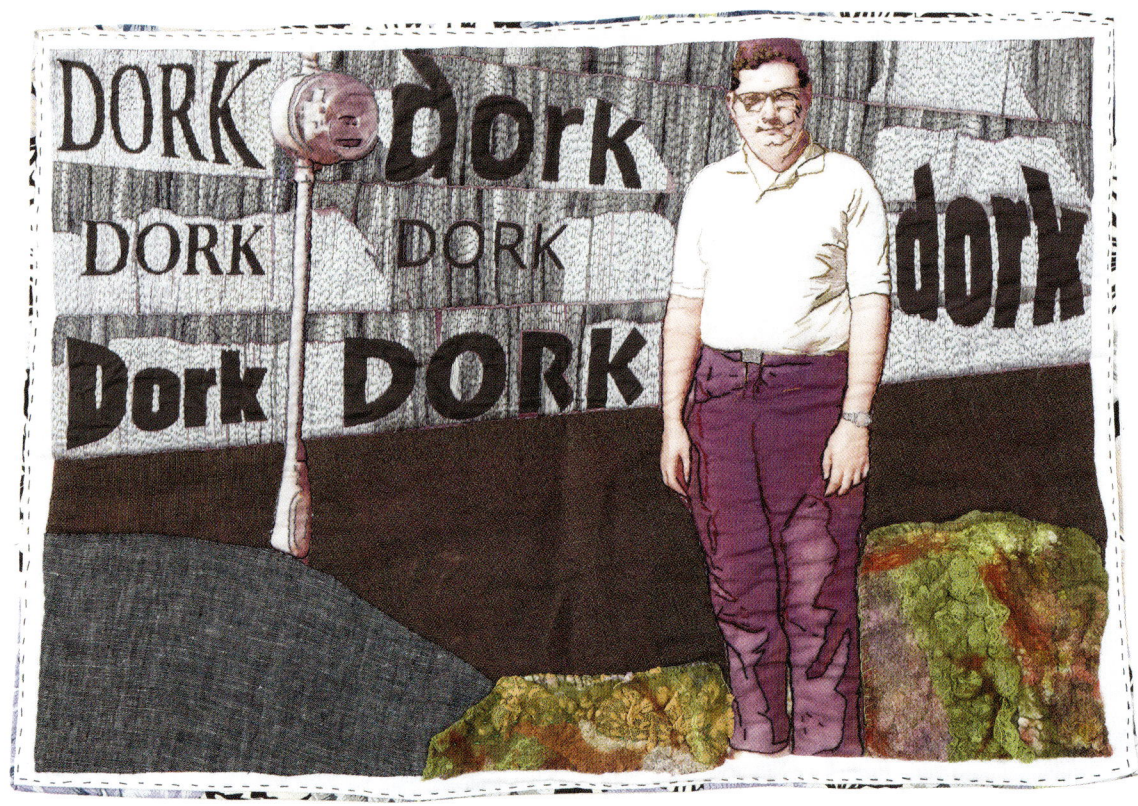

AL KRUEGER
Lake Villa, Illinois

Self Portrait As a Young Dork
18″ x 27″

Pima cotton, linen, silk ribbon, cotton and silk embroidery floss, thread

Photo transfer to fabric, appliqué, hand embroidery, hand quilting

My family has always enjoyed looking over old snapshots, marveling at how we looked in these photos. Many of them include outdated hair and clothing. We laugh a lot. My oldest sister gave me a small album filled with such pictures for my birthday one year. It includes photos of me ranging from childhood to adulthood, many of them quite embarrassing. I decided to celebrate these awkward moments through embroidery and quilting.

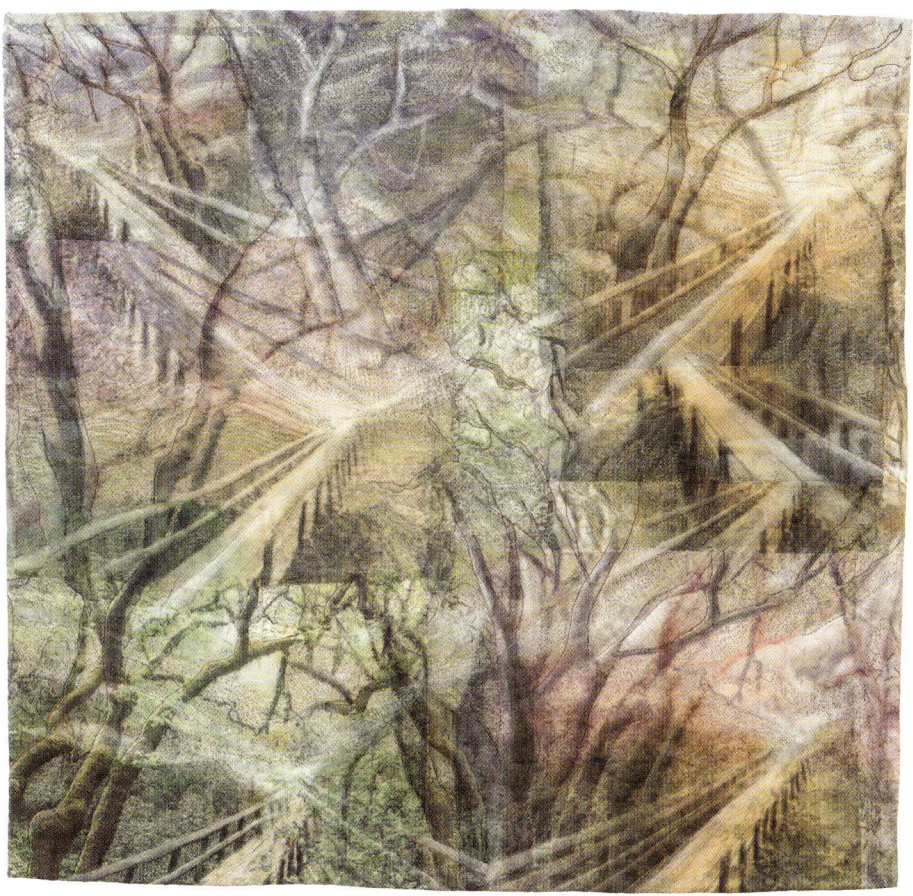

BETTY LACY
Ukiah, California

Mystree One
20″ x 21″

Organza, fusible web, cotton, Inktense pencils, thread

Digital manipulation and coloration, fused, machine quilted

Initially a group challenge to compose a quilt from one's surroundings, I chose the image of bridges near Lake Mendocino. The many twists and turns are reflective of the physical and emotional walking in the face of Alzheimer's disease. Early on in the disease my mother said, "There is nothing I can be certain of." Reluctantly, I began to cross over to her world. The bridges provide a link, expanding and growing despite darkness that follows like a shadow.

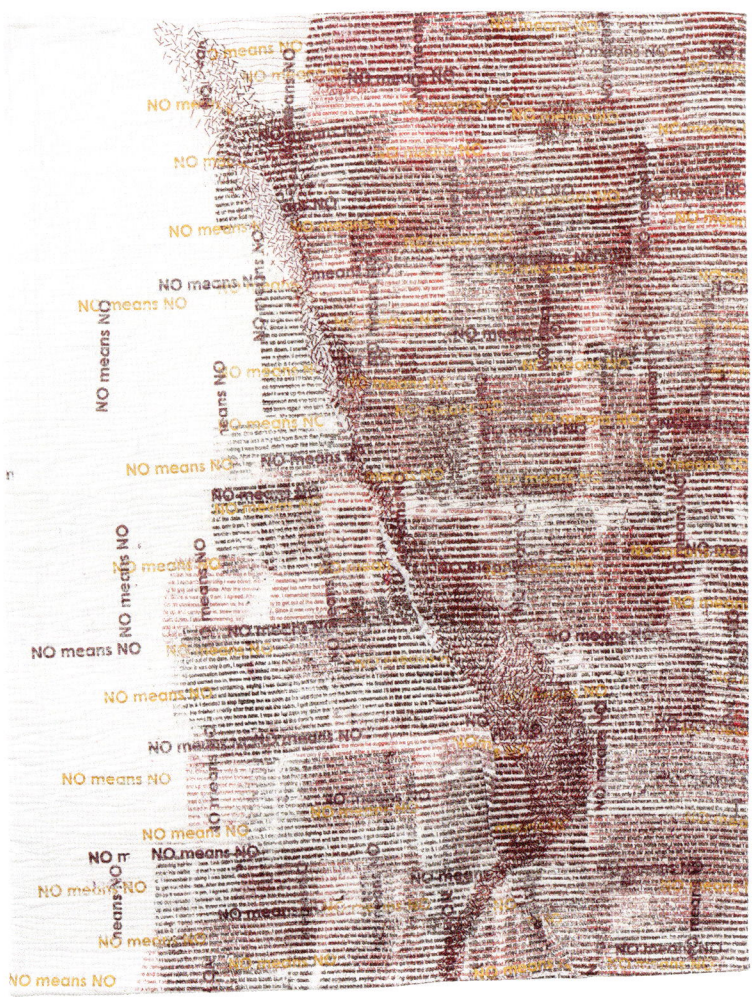

CAROL LARSON
Petaluma, California

Defining Moments 12: NO Means NO
49″ x 39″

Cotton sateen, Perle cotton floss, textile paint

Screen-printed text, machine stitched, hand stitched

The story of my 1967 campus rape is printed to the cloth. The slash represents how this aggressive act disrupted my sense of personal safety and wellbeing. The lenient sentence granted to a Stanford swimmer/rapist in 2016 unearthed my long-repressed shame and anger about my unreported attack. The hand stitching reflects my rage that this insidious behavior continues today and that rapists continue to get away with it, leaving the survivor forever scarred.

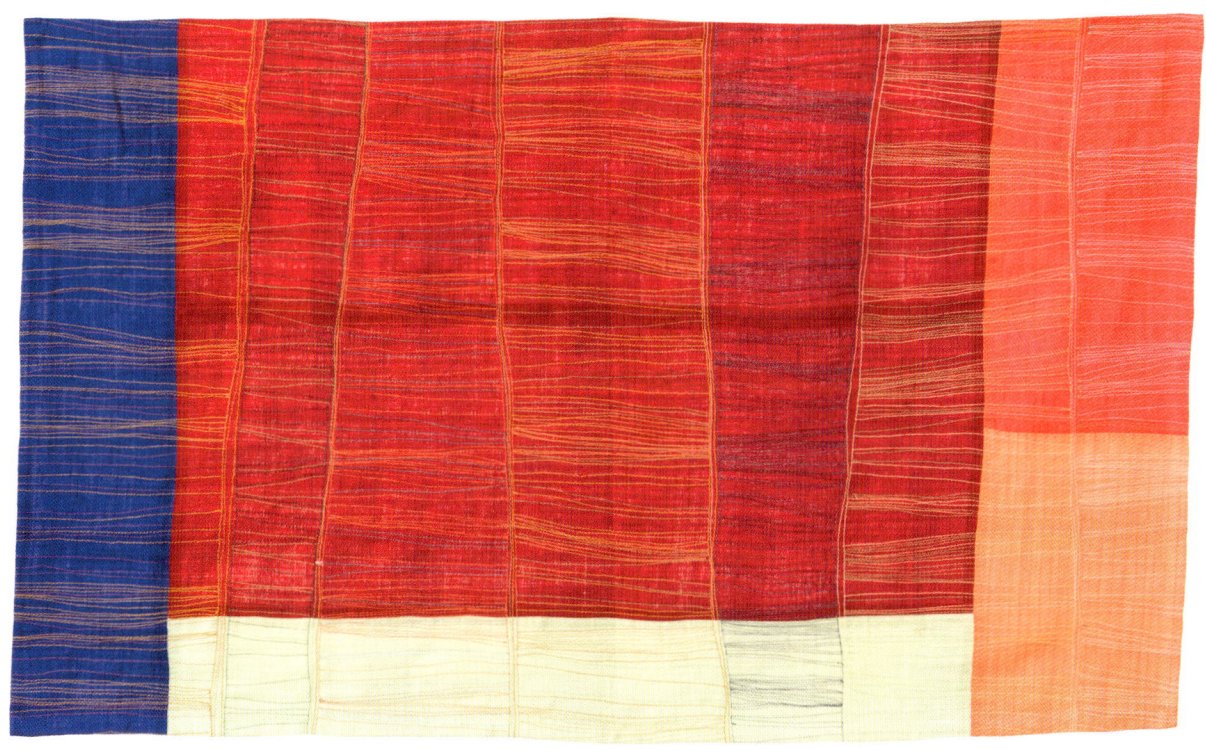

JEEYEUN LEE
Wilmette, Illinois

Speaking Across Borders
30″ x 51″

Ramie with cotton thread

Machine pieced and quilted

For my work in ramie, I draw on the tradition of bojagi, Korean wrapping cloths made from scraps. Like other quilting and piecing traditions, these textiles were made for common household use, but they reference sophisticated aesthetic qualities of abstraction, geometrical form, play of color, and improvisational structure. I highlight these aspects in my work while also adding layers of stitching to add dimension and texture.

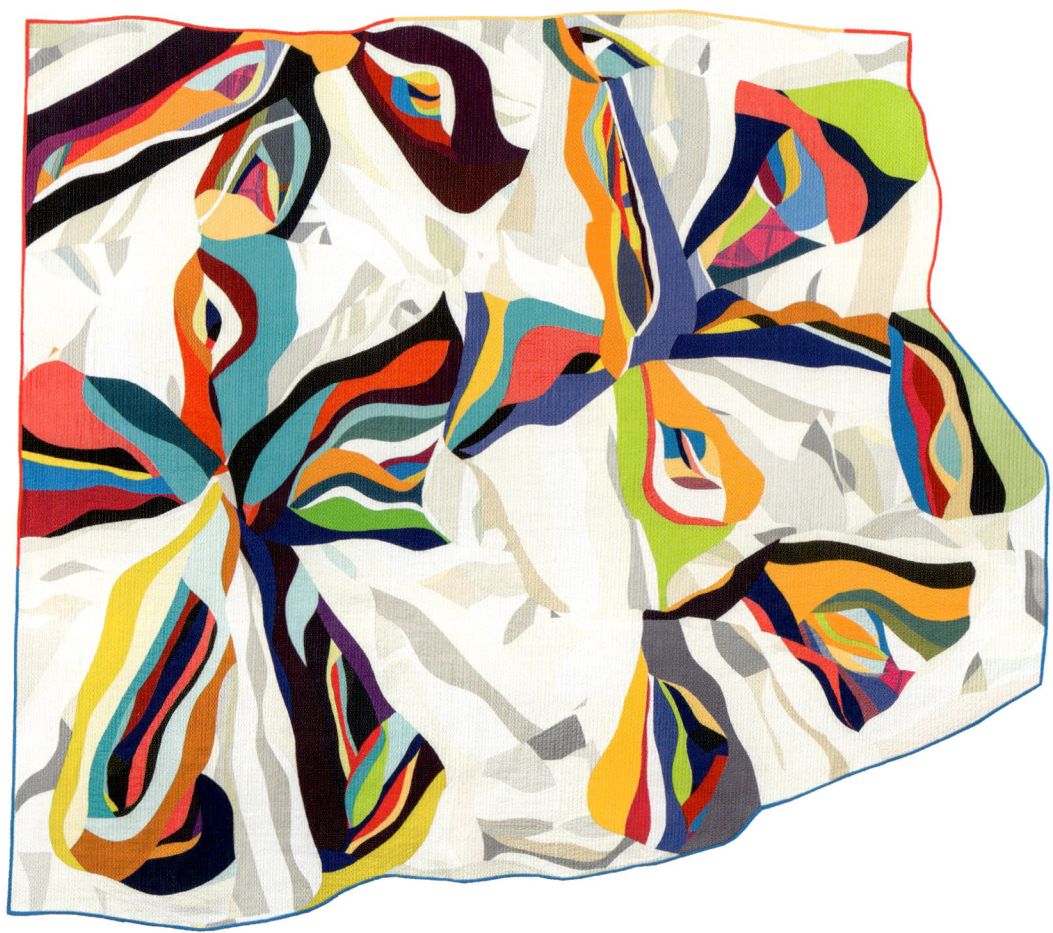

LYNNE LEE
Toronto, Ontario, Canada

From the East to the West
81" x 96"

Commercial cottons

Machine pieced and quilted

Beginning with the Chinese character for big, which brings to mind those of my family that have come before and recognizes those that will carry on, and then quickly morphs into an "Inukshuk," which points the way forward. It's the blending of two lands. It becomes clear that the winds of change and time lead us all in different directions, creating new and ever-evolving experiences that we can't foresee or predict, but always providing a sense of adventure and surprise as life unfolds. So, too, is the development of the quilt!

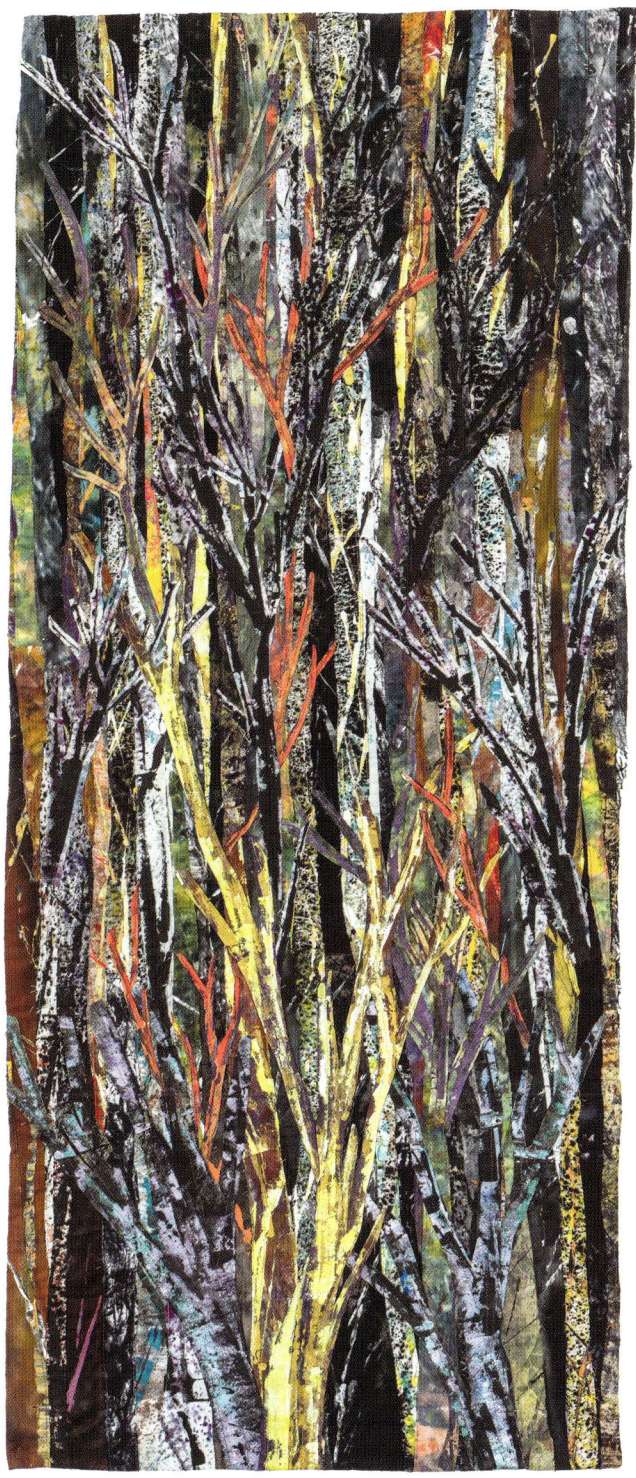

LINDA LEVIN
Wayland,
Massachusetts

Through the Window III
50″ x 20″

Cotton fabric,
textile paints, colored
pencils, thread

Textile painted, layered,
stitched, raw edges

My quilts are made with fabrics which I paint myself to achieve effects that I couldn't obtain otherwise and that create a spontaneity and freshness that purchased fabrics don't provide. Although the inspiration for my work comes from my surroundings, stored away in my memory, I try to capture not a specific scene, but an atmosphere, a mood, or a moment. For me, the tactile qualities of the fabric, the light and shadow created by seams and raw edges, and the interplay of colors provides endless opportunities for exploration.

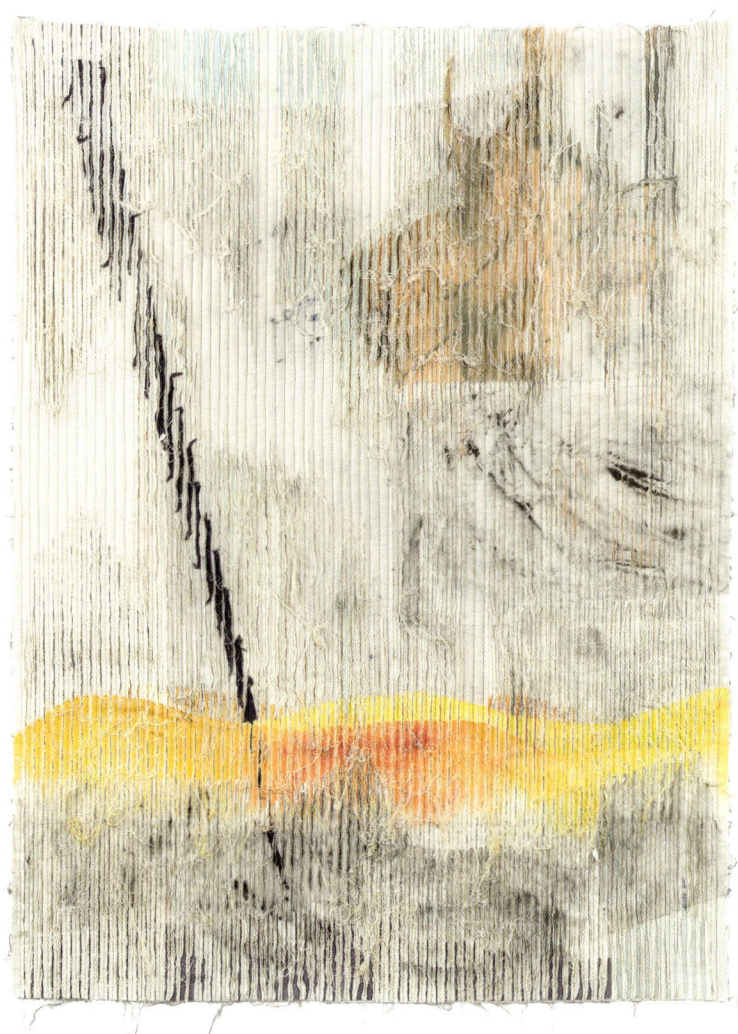

SHULAMIT LISS
Yokneajm, Moshava, Israel

Bright Horizon in Cloudy Sky
57.5″ x 44″

Cotton fabrics, cotton polyester batting

Hand dyed, mono-type printed, discharged, cut, machine stitched

Sunsets differ by colors and dramatic effects, depending on seasons, weather, and colors of sky and sea. One winter evening I experienced a special, beautiful sunset, formed by the contrast of sky and sea and the bright light band between them. This view brought up the thought that at the end of cloudy times in life, there is a hope for light. Nature may join our soul and finds an expression in our artistic work.

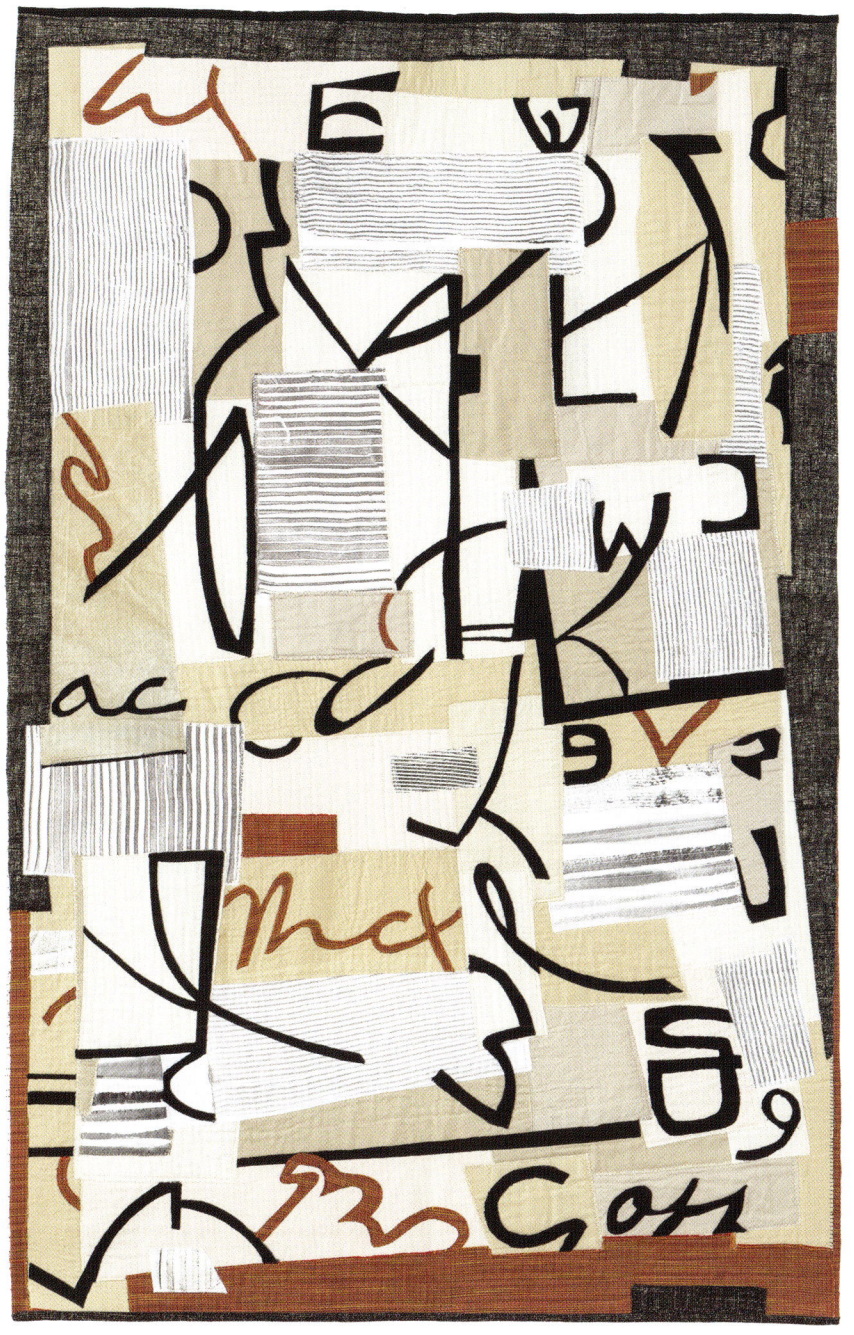

VIVIANA LOMBROZO
San Diego,
California

Building Blocks
44″ x 29″

Commercial and
hand-printed
cotton fabric,
batting, thread

Machine pieced,
appliquéd,
and quilted

*Letters are the
building blocks
of language and
communication,
yet we have to
interpret their
meaning in
the context of
a larger whole.*

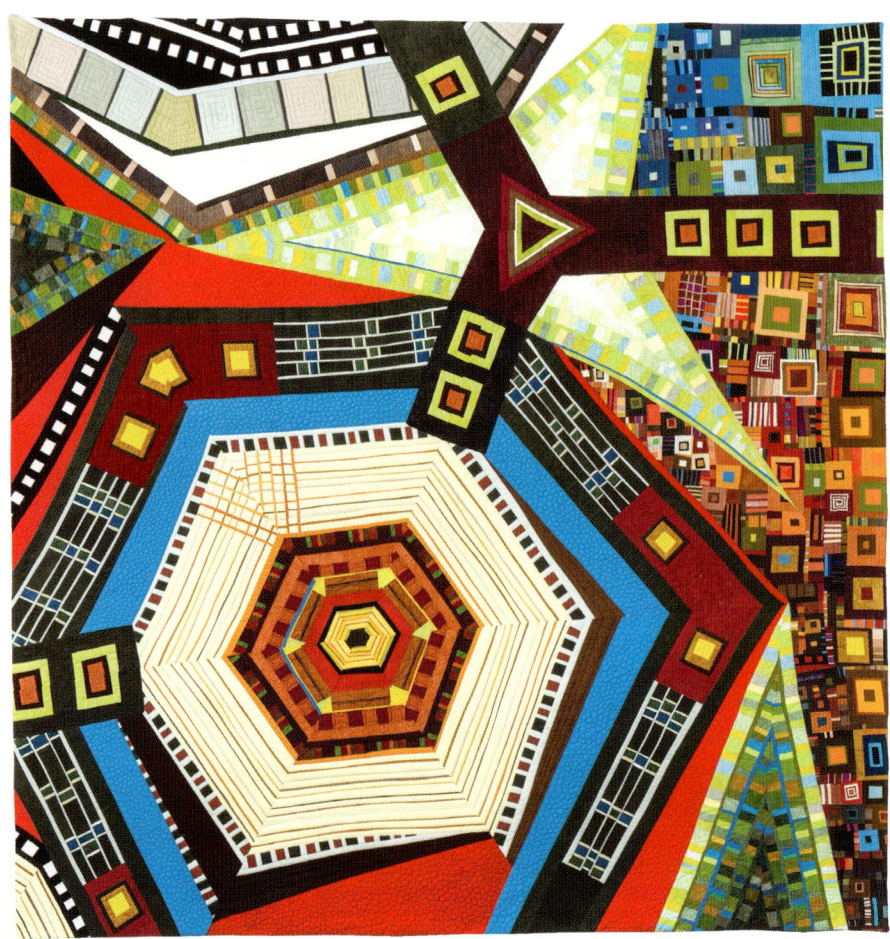

NIRAJA LORENZ
Eugene, Oregon

Strange Attractor #16
82″ x 82″

Hand-dyed and commercial cotton fabric

Improvisationally designed, machine pieced and quilted

Strange Attractor #16 is pieced entirely of solid colored fabric. Subtle variations in color, intricate piecing, and organic textures inspire the creation of ever unfolding visual imagery as I explore the interface between regular patterning and apparent randomness. Mathematics and Chaos Theory describe an "attractor" as that which pulls you toward it. A "strange" attractor has a fractal structure, a repeating pattern on every scale. This is the largest attractor I have constructed.

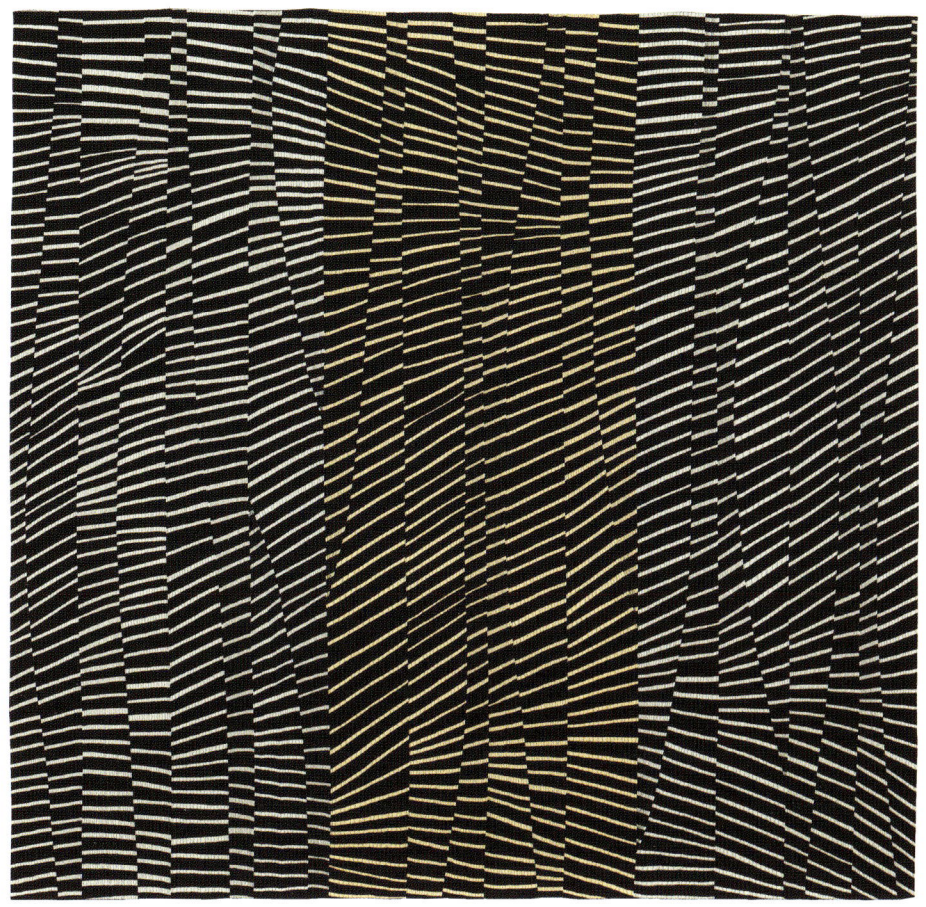

VALERIE MASER-FLANAGAN
Carlisle, Massachusetts

Inner Thoughts Inner Rhythm
65" x 68"

Hand-dyed cotton fabric, commercial cotton
fabric, cotton batting, cotton thread

Dyed, freely cut lines and shapes, improvisational
construction, machine pieced and quilted

*Inner Thoughts Inner Rhythm is part of a series that
focuses on a growing awareness of my own internal process.*

AMY MEISSNER

Anchorage, Alaska

Fatigue Threshold

70" x 54"

Abandoned quilt top, child's bed sheet, silk organza, vintage wool, vintage upholstery, vintage crocheted doilies, cotton embroidery floss, cotton batting

Machine pieced, hand appliquéd, hand embroidered, hand quilted and finished

In materials study, "fatigue" refers to a component's failure after repeated and excessive loads—the crumpled beam, the snapped lever, the bowed wall. This piece explores the landscape of women's work through the use of abandoned cloth, the female form, and traditional handwork, portraying the moment before collapse. The burdens are emotional, physical, sexual, literal. We hoard, discard, mend, and make do because despite our destruction some scrap of beauty can always be salvaged.

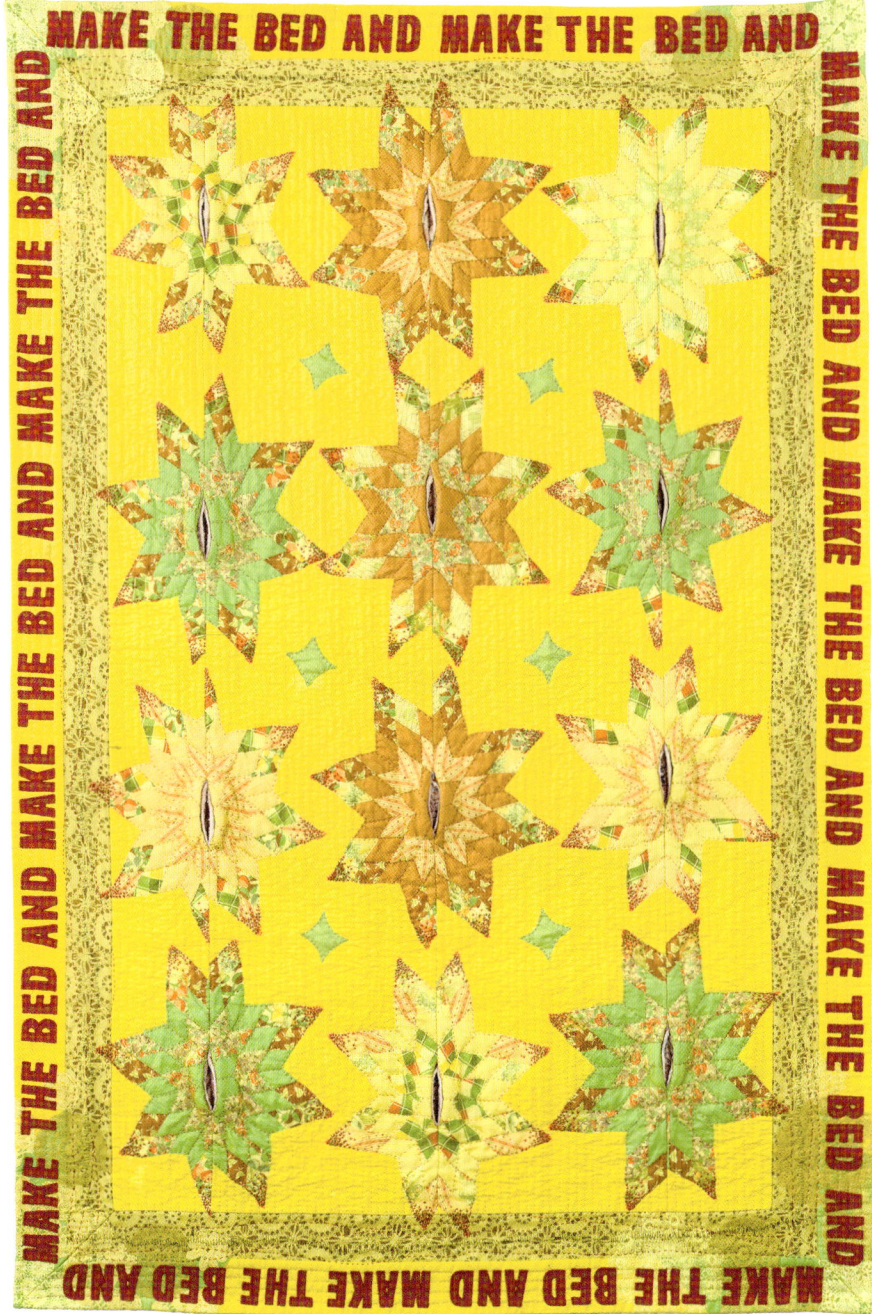

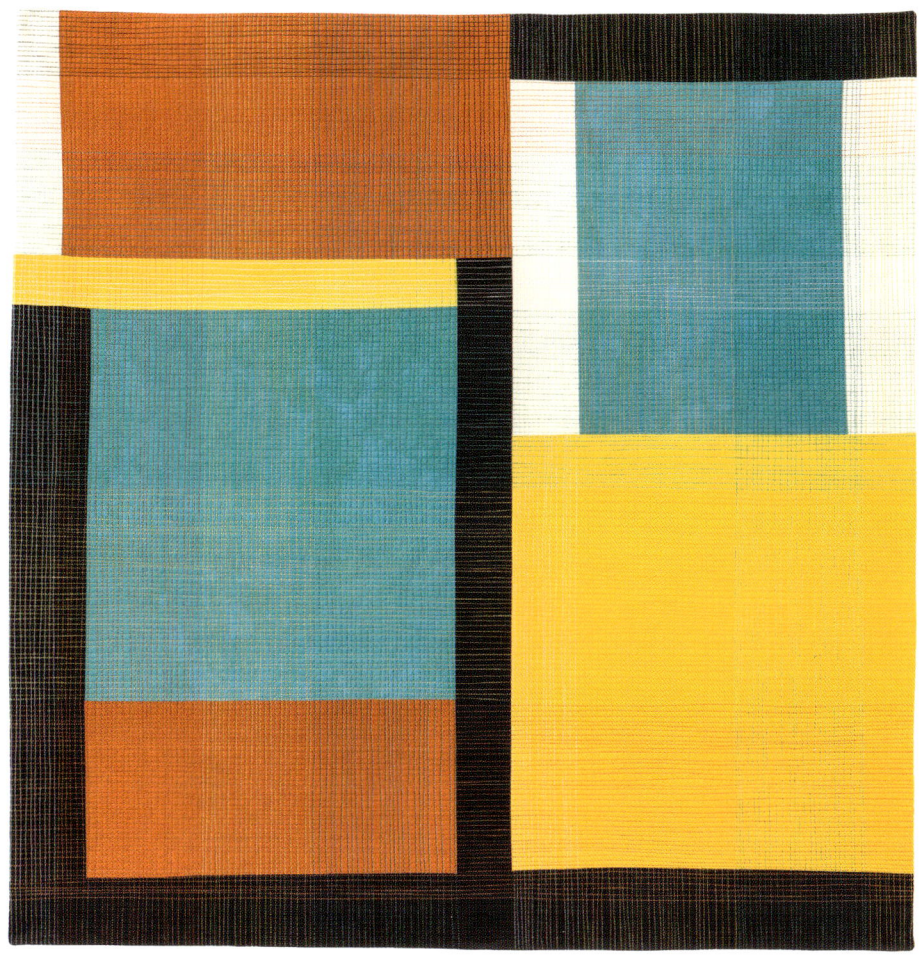

BARBARA NEPOM
Lopez Island, Washington

Corners of My Mind 2
35″ x 35″

Hand-dyed cotton sateen, cotton batting, cotton thread

Hand dyed, machine pieced, hand quilted

Sometimes an idea seems to arise unbidden from the recesses of our minds.

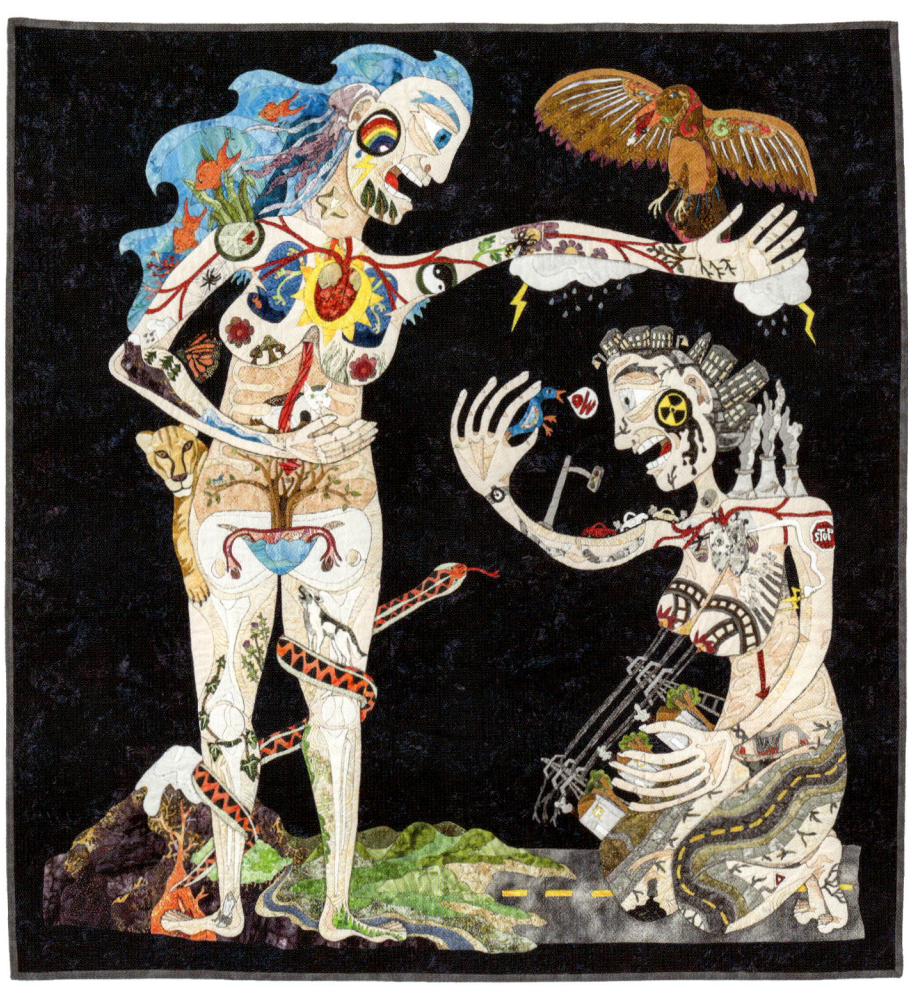

KATHY NIDA
El Cajon, California

Beyond the Concrete
58″ x 59″

Hand-dyed and commercial cottons, ink

Fused appliqué, machine stitched and quilted, inked

*I want Mother Nature to win, not concrete and asphalt crawling all over my
Earth, the hills, flowers, trees, stifling insects or birds, scaring off wolves and lions.
I want Mother Nature to stand up, throw off the cement sidewalks and electrical
transmission towers, let weeds grow in cracks and roads crumble to dirt. I want her
to stand up and yell at what humans have wrought upon her. I want her to win big.*

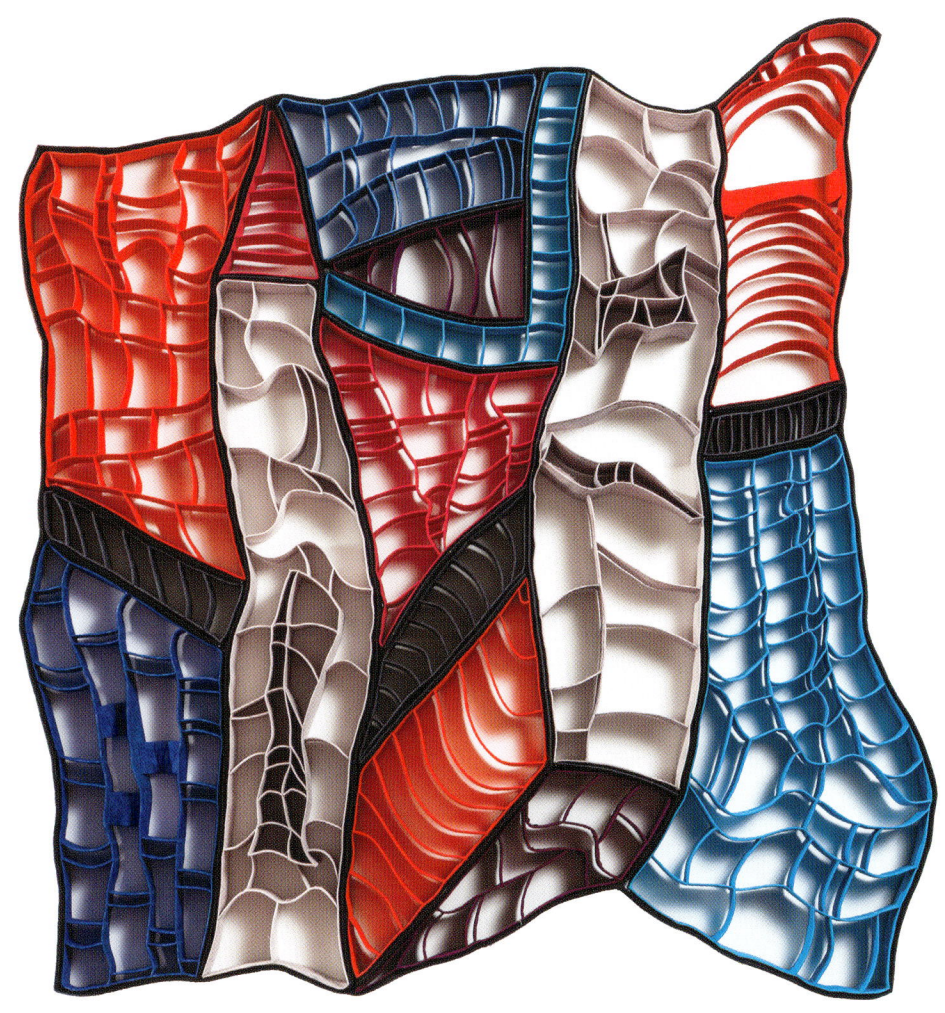

DIANE NÚÑEZ
Southfield, Michigan

Cinque Terre
49″ x 49″ x 3″

Hand-dyed cotton fabric, batting, thread, hook and loop tape

Whole fabric assembled and quilted

Cinque Terre is inspired by the unique three-dimensional forms found along the Italian Riviera. Colorful coastal cities perched along steep slopes with many colorful homes and buildings. The rectilinear forms and angles are reflected here; the black connections represent the connections, the circulation patterns of walks and roads. As the light hits the work, look at the reflections and shadows that are formed.

DAN OLFE
Julian, California

San Diego Courthouse #1

70″ x 40″

Polyester fabric,
polyester batting,
cotton canvas,
cotton thread

Photoshop to modify
and layer three photos,
digitally-printed,
machine quilted

To design this quilt, I started with three photos I took of a new white courthouse in San Diego. I used Photoshop to modify and layer the images to create the final design. It is not surprising that the quilt resembles a Bauhaus weaving, because the courthouse architect Richard Meier carries on the Bauhaus tradition with his modernist designs that feature grid and stripe patterns.

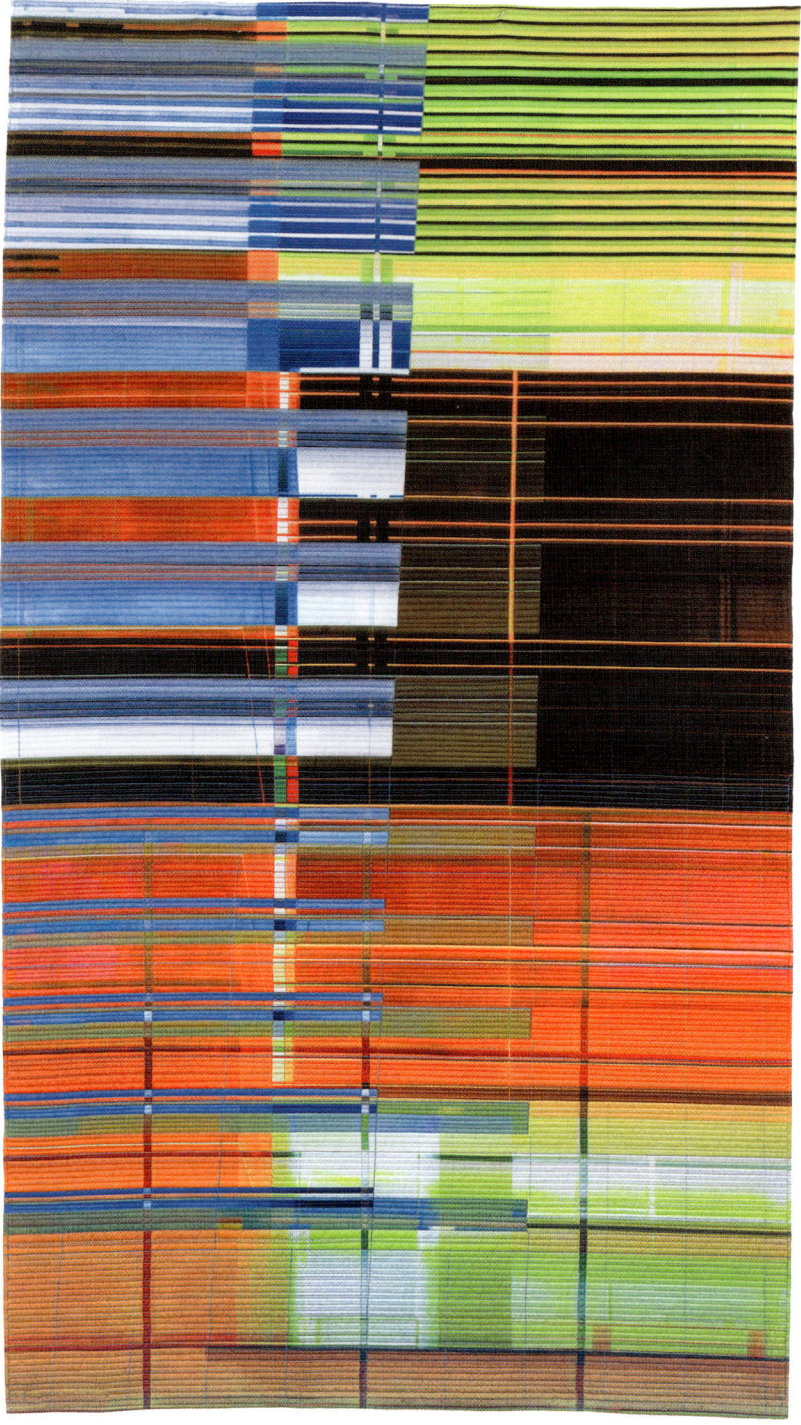

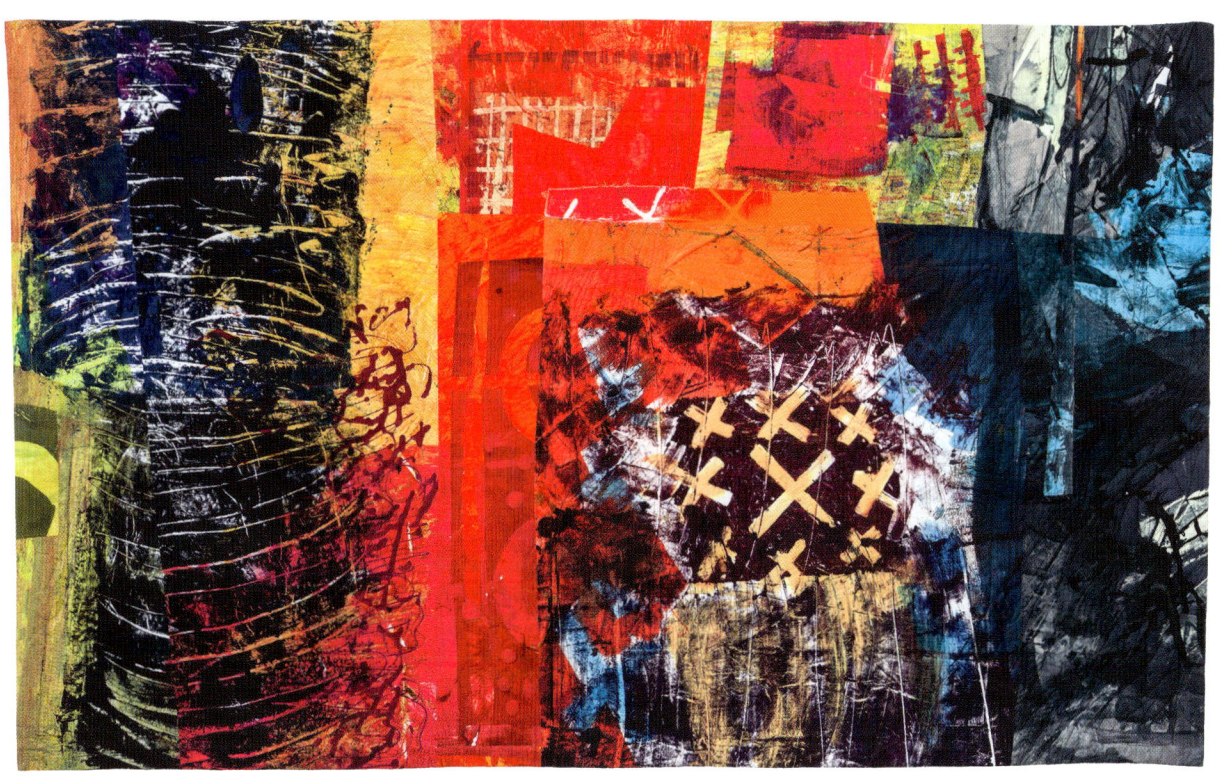

PAT PAULY
Rochester, New York

Normandy
55″ x 92″

Cotton, wool, synthetic fiber

Pieced, raw edge appliquéd, mono-printed, screen printed, direct dye painted

The explosive use of surface design techniques, at least with large-scale printing and direct dyeing, informed the subject matter. I leave the viewer to find relationships among the images. Normandy needed to be high chroma, for certain. But I didn't have to spell out the particulars.

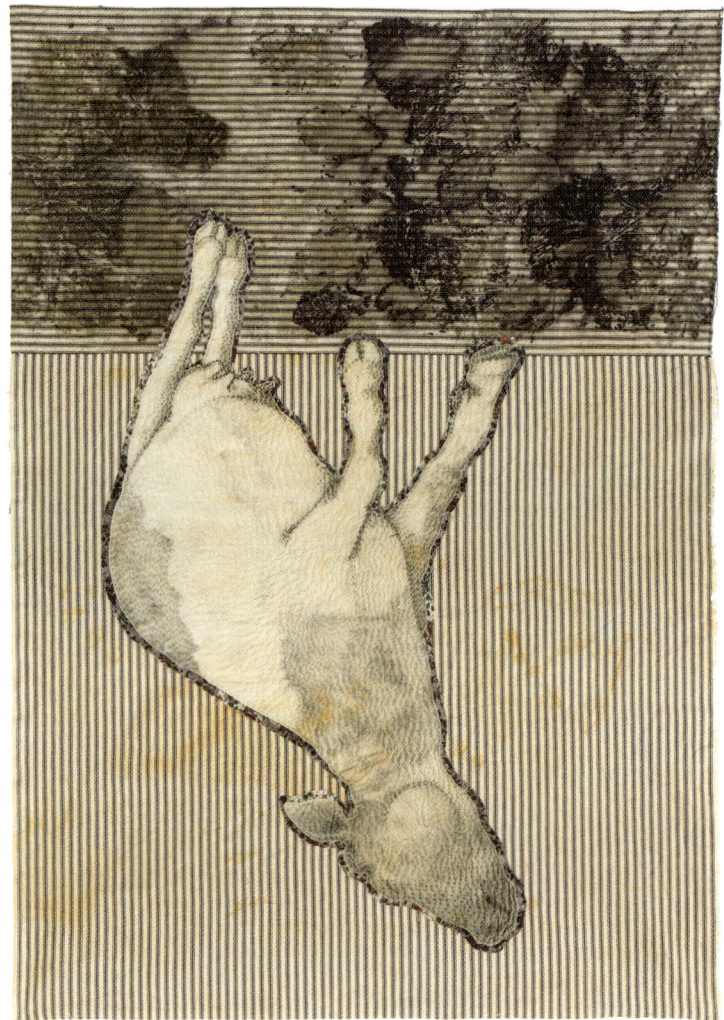

DANETTE PRATT
Coolville, Ohio

Meadow Memories: Study II, Summer Walk 2016
44″ x 31.5″

Cotton fabrics, laser print transfer, pencil, carbon dust, and charcoal, collected field plants, tree and shrub leaves

Plant-dyed fabric, hand stitched, raw edges, thread knots

My practice involves research that addresses the subtle prompts that evoke memory. My research utilizes the mediums of plants dyes, photo transfer, drawing tools (pencil, carbon dust, ink), assorted embroidery/ quilting techniques onto selected paper and fabric to suggest recall and commemoration. The work is intended to provoke contemplation of the past.

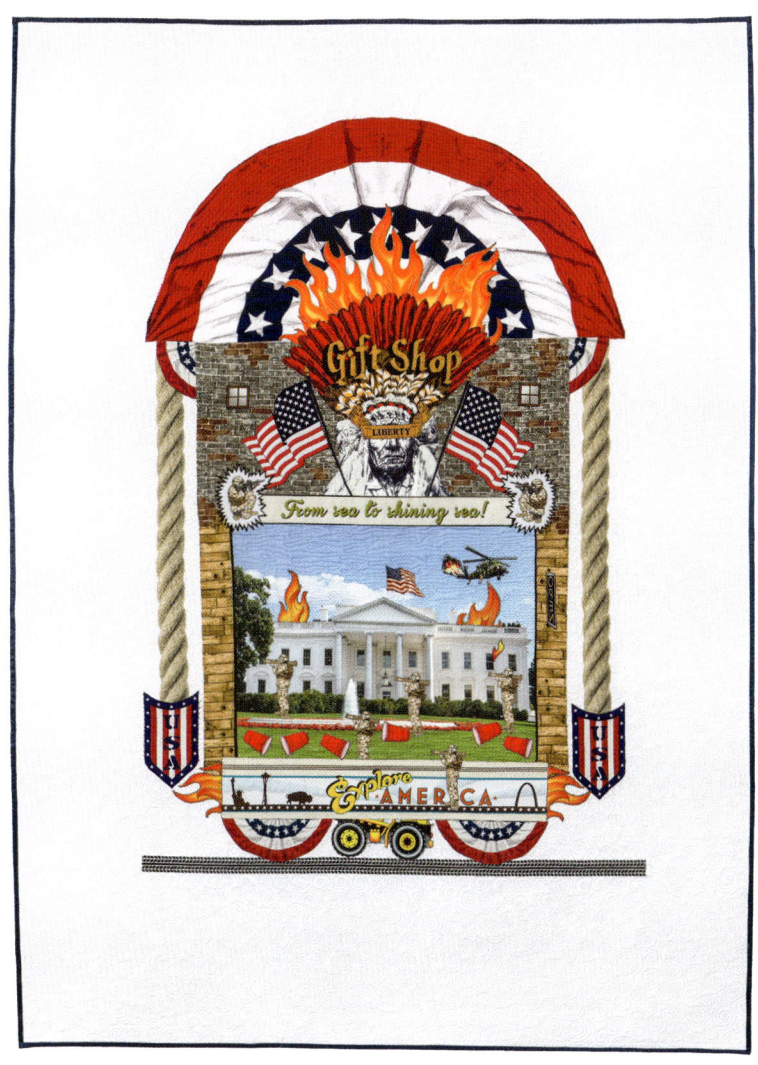

SHAWN QUINLAN
Pittsburgh, Pennsylvania

Explore America
72″ x 53″

Cotton fabrics, batting, thread

Pieced, appliquéd, machine quilted

The content, as in many of my quilts, is loosely based on subjects such as hypocrisy, corruption, self-righteousness, and contradiction. I see how these characteristics so often hide behind religion, propaganda, and the like.

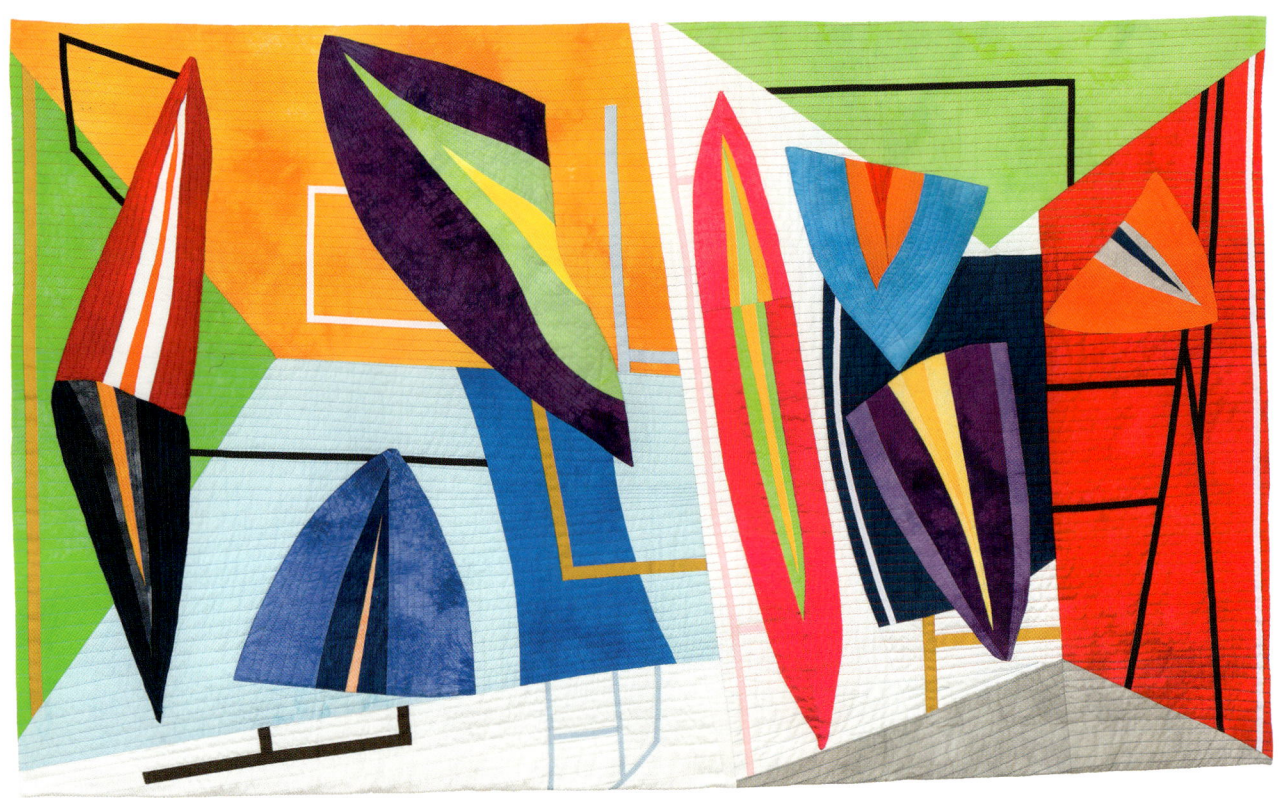

DAREN REDMAN
Nashville, Indiana

Indiana Flowers
41″ x 70″

Cottons, vintage and new grosgrain ribbon, cotton batting, polyester backing

Cottons hand dyed with fiber-reactive dyes, rotary cut
intuitively, machine pieced and quilted, machine appliquéd

*I make quilted wall hangings from my hand-dyed fabrics representing abstract
landscapes. The endless number of colors in the leaves, grasses, tree trunks, and
mosses in the Indiana landscape is a constant inspiration. Nature and my travels
are a recurring theme in my work. I take water conservation and recycling seriously
when hand-dyeing silks and cottons in my studio in Brown County, Indiana.*

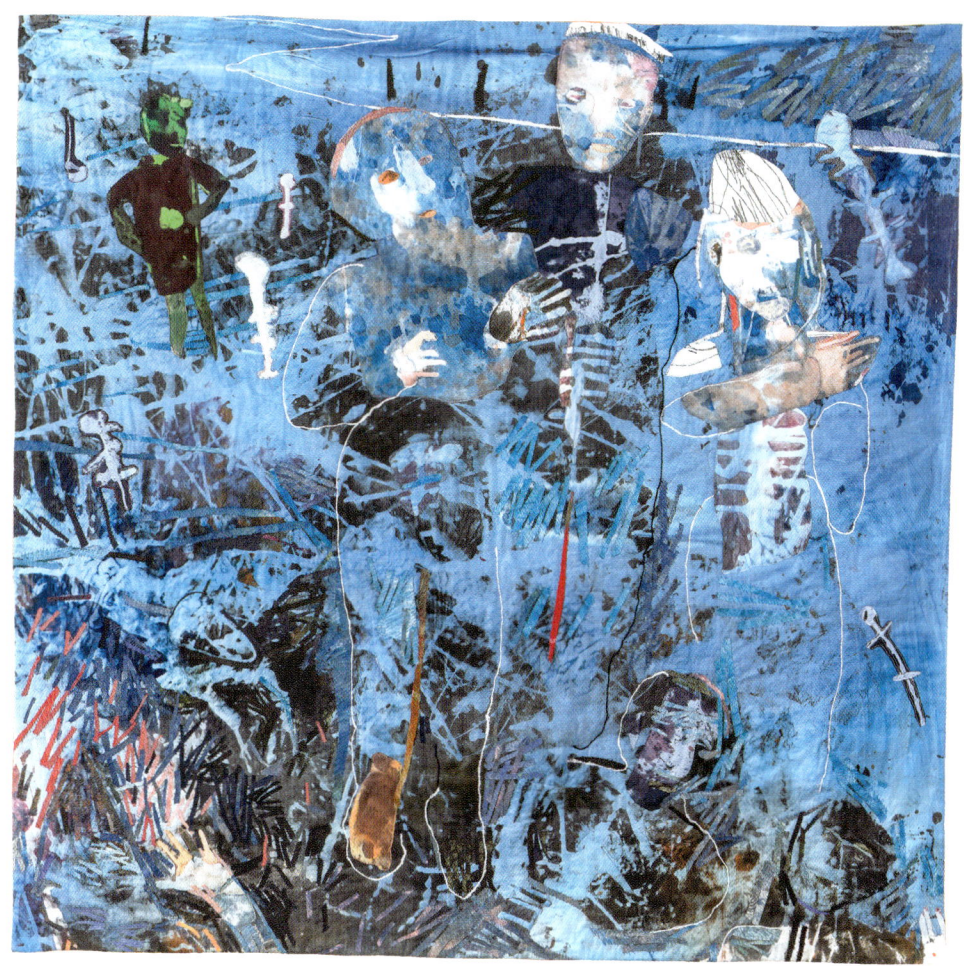

DINAH SARGEANT
Newhall, California

Spines Return
48.5″ x 50″

Painted cotton, canvas, embroidery thread

Hand-painted cotton and canvas, machine appliquéd, machine quilted

I got my spine back.

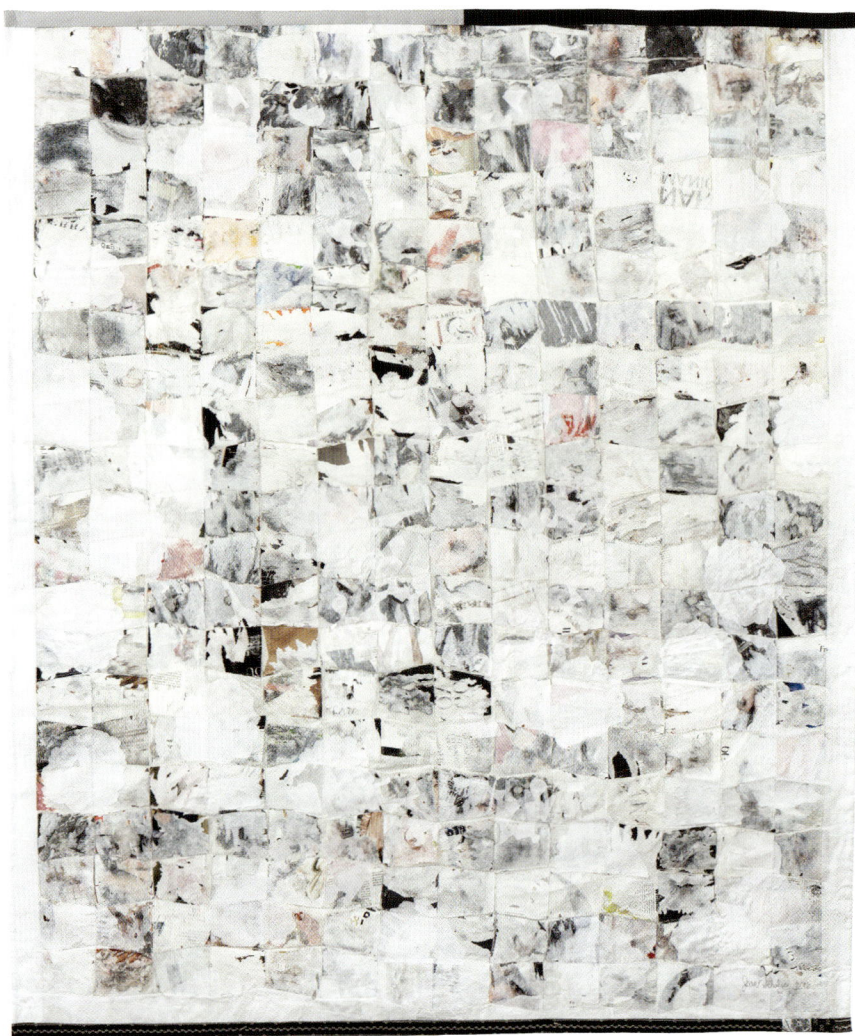

JOAN SCHULZE
Sunnyvale, California

Carpet
65″ x 56″

Silk, paper, cotton

Glue transfer (paper to silk), fused appliquéd, machine stitched and quilted

*Carpet/a white composition/clinging to gnarled branches/releases a wild and playful
flurry of petals/a dancer's waltz catching the wind/plum blossoms signal/the warming
days of spring/transitioning from white to green/hiding hints of edible burgundy*

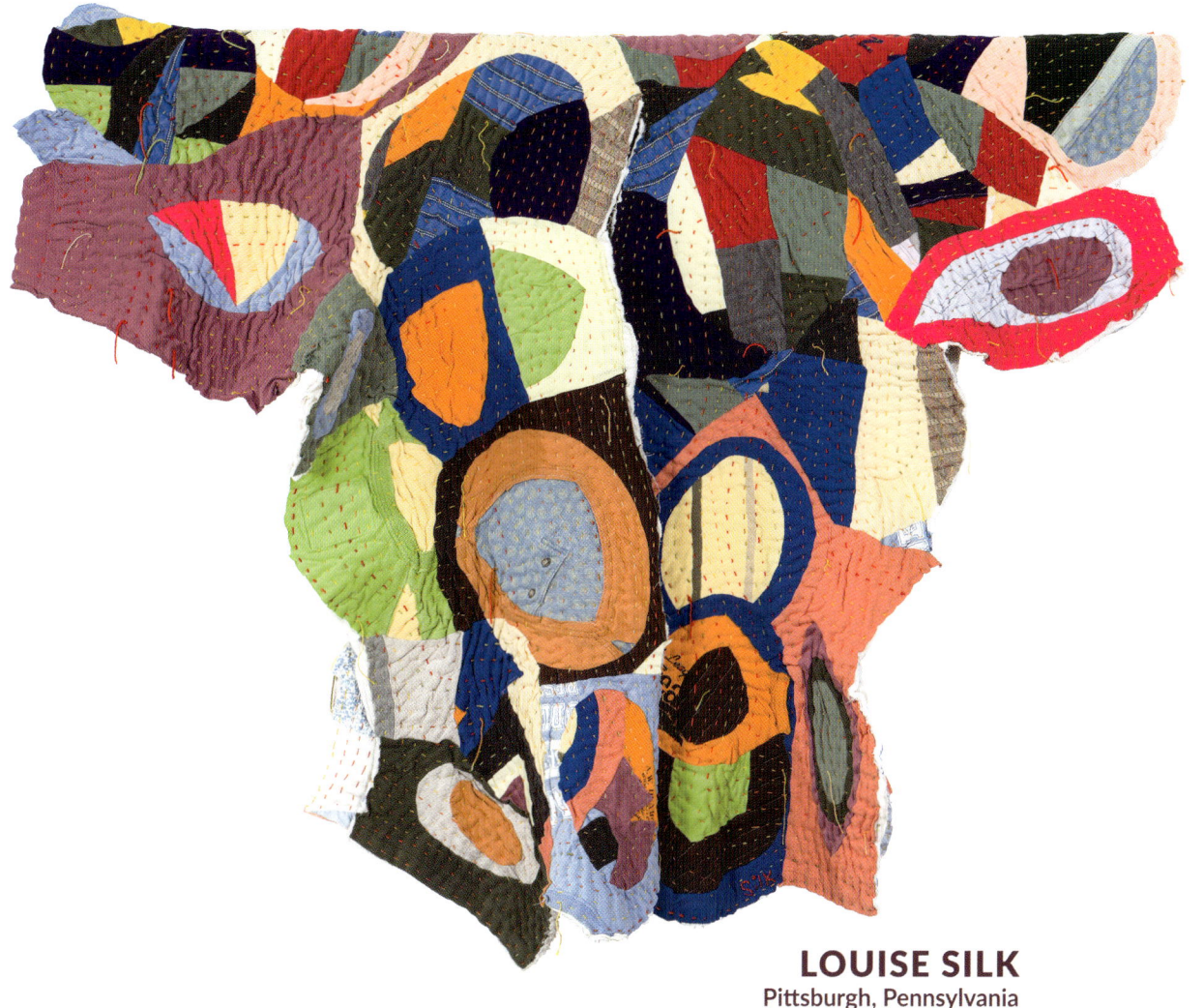

LOUISE SILK
Pittsburgh, Pennsylvania

Rasiel's Mantle
43" x 63"

Knit tee-shirt remnants, Perle cotton, wool yarn, old quilt

Machine pieced, hand quilted

This work is composed of ordinary re-used materials. The archangel, Rasiel, presides over our actions of transforming the knowledge of information and ideas into the wisdom of achieving our deepest levels of understanding. The mantle, like a quilt, serves the practical function of keeping someone warm, protecting them from the elements. In this case, it also serves as a symbolic divine representation.

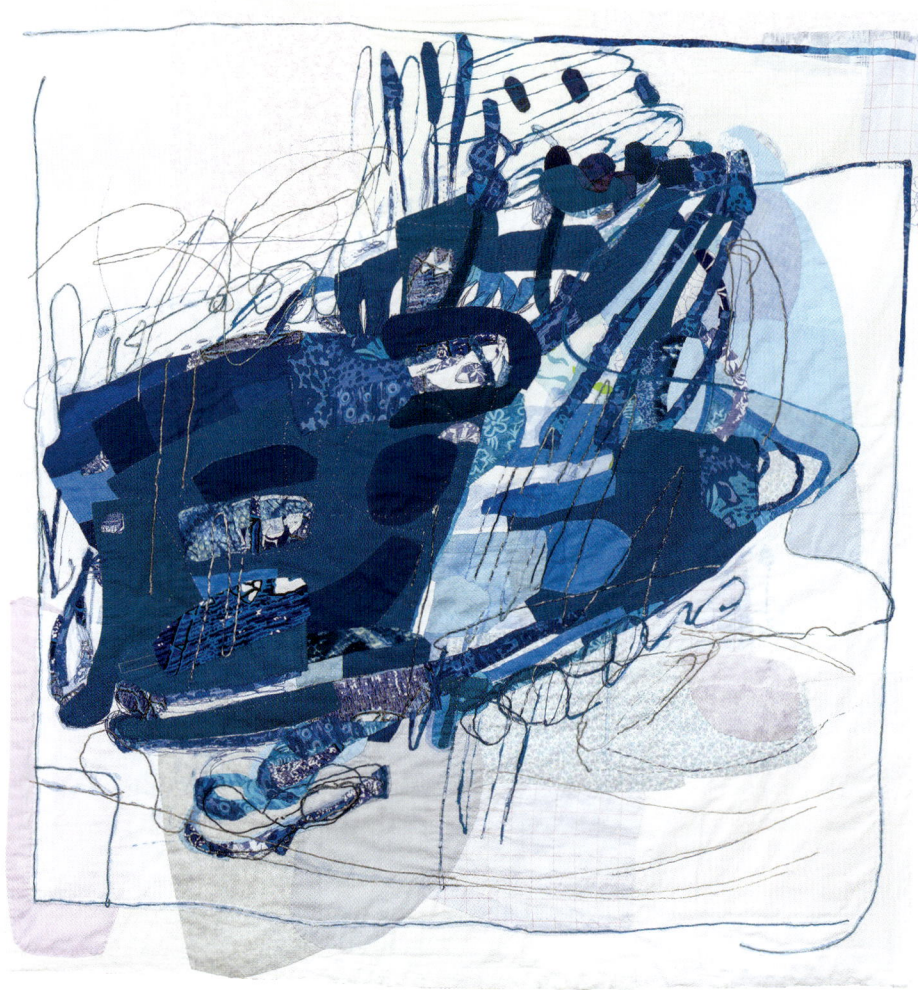

ANNE SMITH
Pontypridd, Wales

Koan
54″ x 56″

Recycled cotton, sewing thread, string

Hand pieced, hand appliquéd, machine embroidered, hand quilted

*"Koan: In Buddhism, a puzzling, often paradoxical statement,
given to students to provoke sudden intuitive enlightenment and
spiritual awakening." This quilt is a further exploration of my interest
in creating movement within the stillness of the quilt form.*

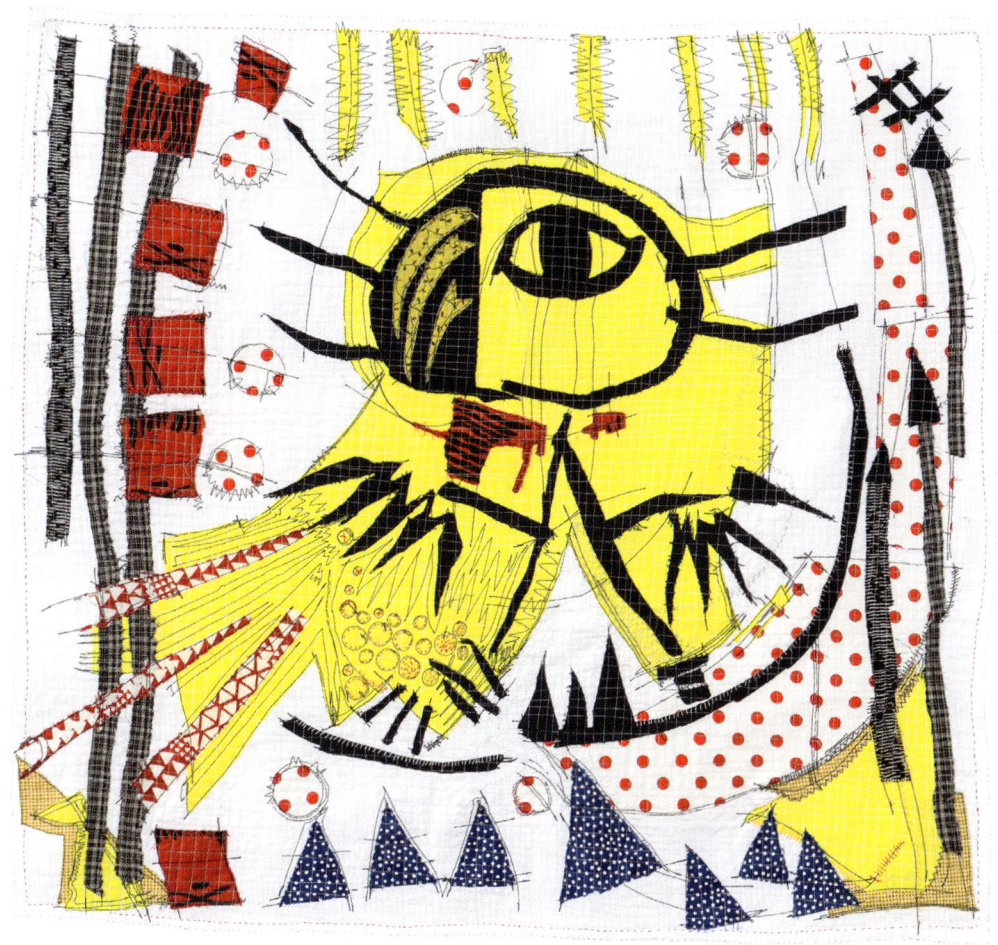

GINNY SMITH
Arlington, Virginia

L'oiseau de Mme Wazoh
38″ x 36″

Feedbag dishtowel, commercial cotton fabric, cotton thread

Hand appliquéd and embroidered, machine appliquéd and quilted

I have been using bird images for many years, some more realistic than others. Mme. Wazoh's bird is a symbol, a heraldic device, a stand-in for all birds, all the individual, varied birds that one encounters in a normal day.

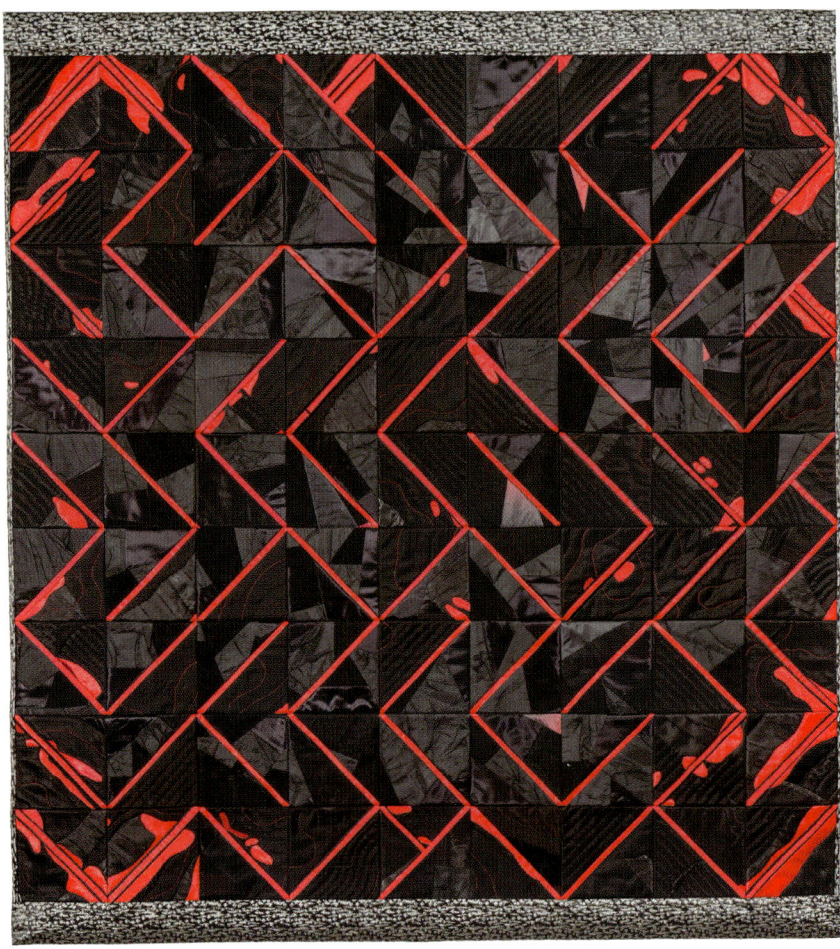

PETRA SOESEMANN
Cleveland Heights, Ohio

Refugee Trilogy: Refugee's Journey
62" x 57"

Silk, cotton, and synthetic fabrics; synthetic and natural batting

Hand and machine pieced and quilted, fused and hand appliquéd

Refugee's Journey is the second quilt in the Refugee Trilogy series. The quilt explores geometric pattern, repetition, color, and texture to create a visually active surface that conveys mood and suggests a narrative. The maze pattern, irregular surface texture, and darker palette all speak to the treacherous reality of a refugee's journey.

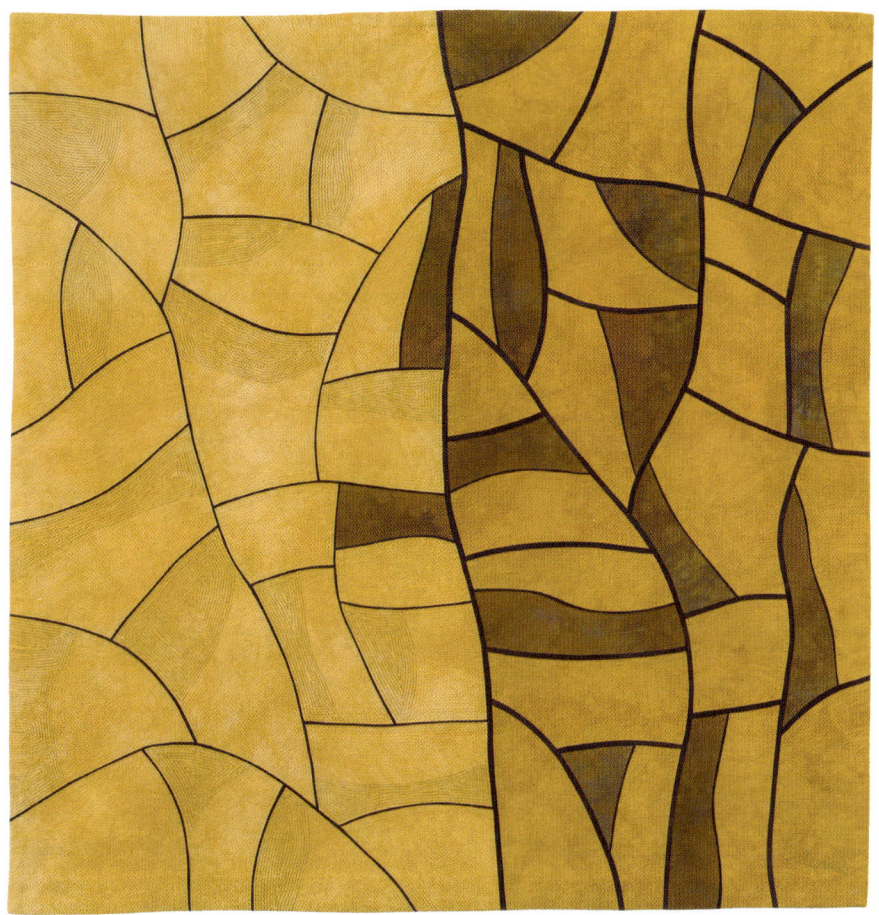

JANET STEADMAN
Langley, Washington

Outliers
38″ x 38″

Hand-dyed cotton, cotton thread, cotton batting, cotton backing

Freehand cut, machine pieced and quilted

While working in a series of fine line quilts involving the graceful lines of trees and branches, I came across a close-up photograph of an unevenly rusted surface. I knew at once I wanted to capture that fractured surface in fabric. I challenged myself to figure out how to construct the image I sought, and eventually developed a new piecing technique as I worked out the idea. The finished piece demonstrates the grace we find in nature when we view it closely.

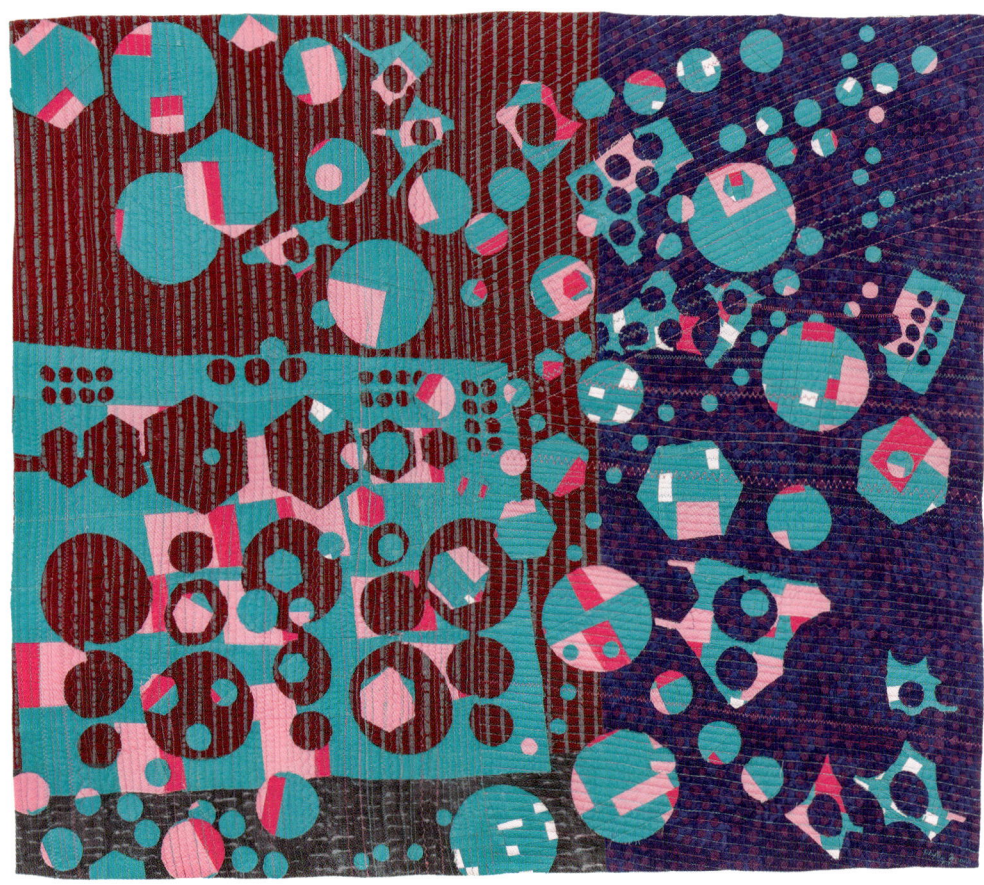

PHYLLIS TARRANT
Matthews, North Carolina

Ode to an AccuQuilt Cutter
38″ x 45″

Commercial cotton fabric, polyester thread, cotton/bamboo batting

Pieced, AccuQuilt Cutter to cut the shapes, raw edge
appliquéd, straight and decorative stitch machine quilted

*My friend, Christine, a traditional quilter, loves her AccuQuilt cutter. She suggested
several times that I might like to use it. Finding two small long-neglected quilt tops proved
to be the solution to this dilemma. Viewers should interpret the meaning based on their
own experiences. To me, the meaning is connected to the design creation process, the
puzzle of making order out of chaos, and like many of my quilts, experimentation and joy.*

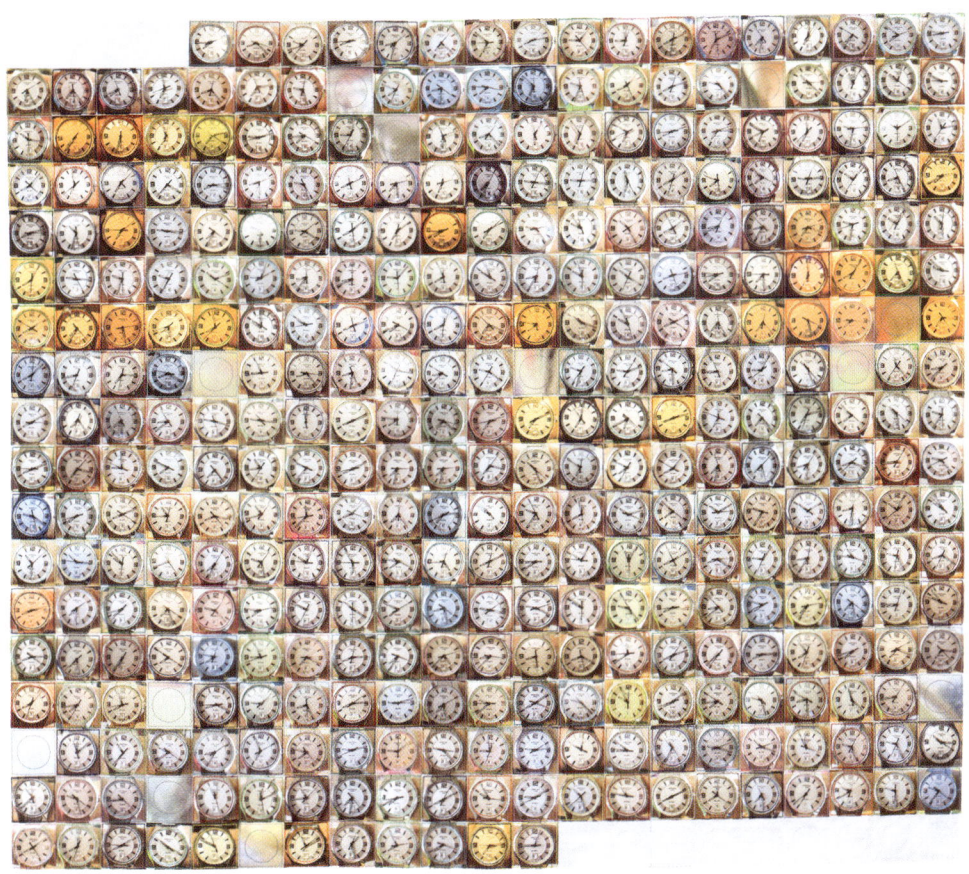

CÉCILE TRENTINI
Zurich, Switzerland

One Year
70″ x 82″

Fabric sheets for inkjet printer, felt, cotton fabric

Photos printed on fabric, fused, machine stitched and quilted

I go walking for at least thirty minutes every day. During a whole year, I recorded the starting time of each walk by taking a picture of my watch. If I skipped my walk, there is no picture of the watch. This is, simultaneously, a means of motivation for my daily exercise, a journal, and a way to literally materialize time and illustrate how much (or how little?) space one year takes on a wall.

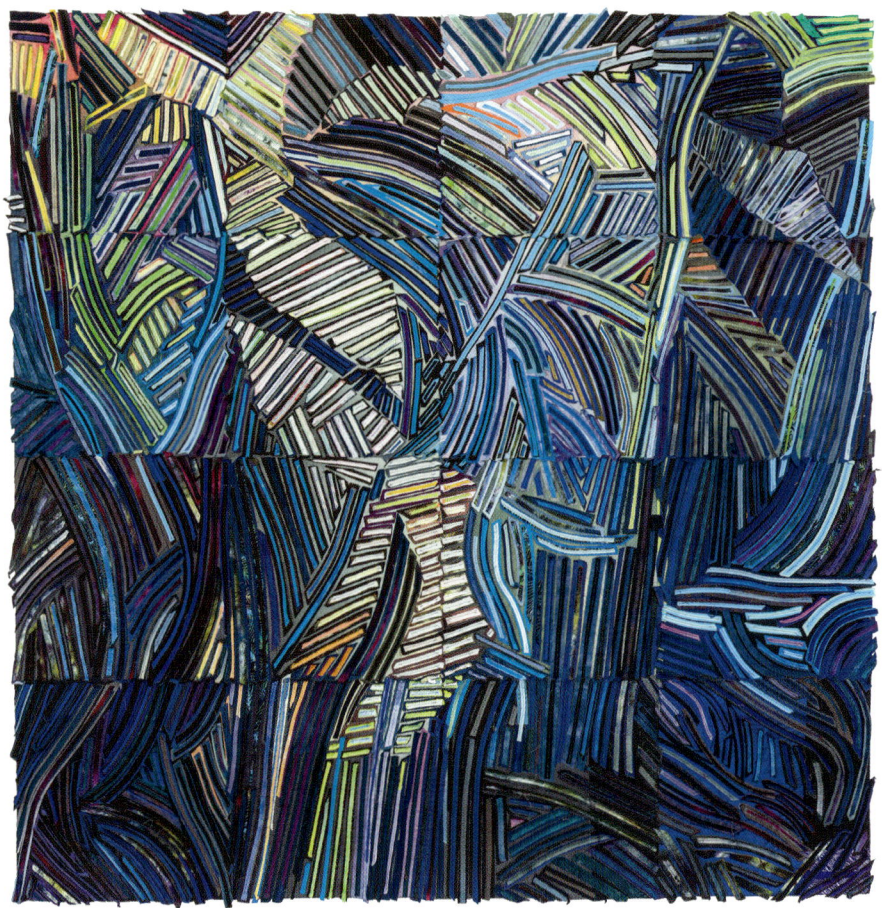

KIT VINCENT
Ottawa, Ontario, Canada

Nightshift
79" x 79"

Cotton, silk, dyed and commercial cottons, cotton, silk
and polyester thread, polyester batting, cotton backing

Machine pieced and quilted, appliquéd

*With this piece, I was excited by the many possibilities offered with these
materials and techniques. I began without expectation, allowing the design to
surface as I worked. Gesture, movement, and color were the focus as I stitched
across these 16 panels with narrow strips of cloth. My goal was to challenge the
perception of this material and to create an emotional response with the viewer.*

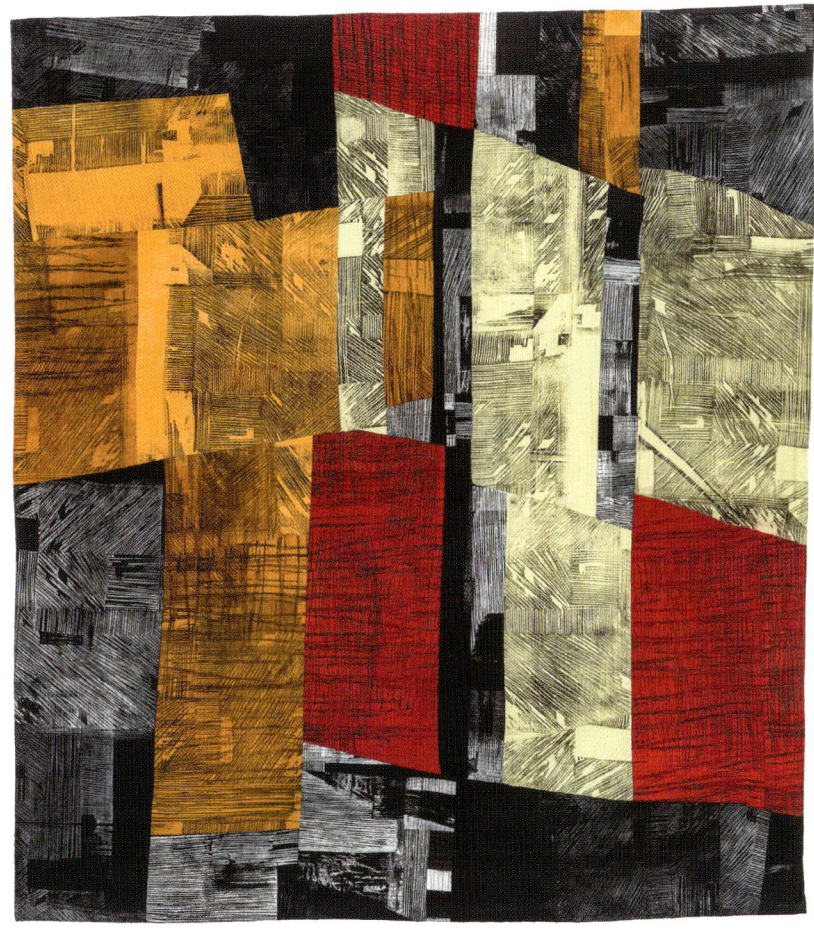

BARB WILLS
Prescott, Arizona

STRUCTURES #5
51″ x 46″

Pimatex cotton, Procion dyes, altered printing dyes/inks, Shina wood woodcuts

Hand-dyed fabric, original Shina woodcuts by hand, woodcut
hand printed on fabrics, machine pieced and quilted

*My artwork is driven by a passion to experiment and create allowing my mark-making
to become my "voice." Inspiration and imagery come from my natural environment of
forests, mountains, rocks, marks on the ground and trails, in the trees, and in the sky.
I translate this imagery into lines, layers, and shapes. Trees and fallen timber become
the abstracted angular figures in my work as they help support my mark-making.*

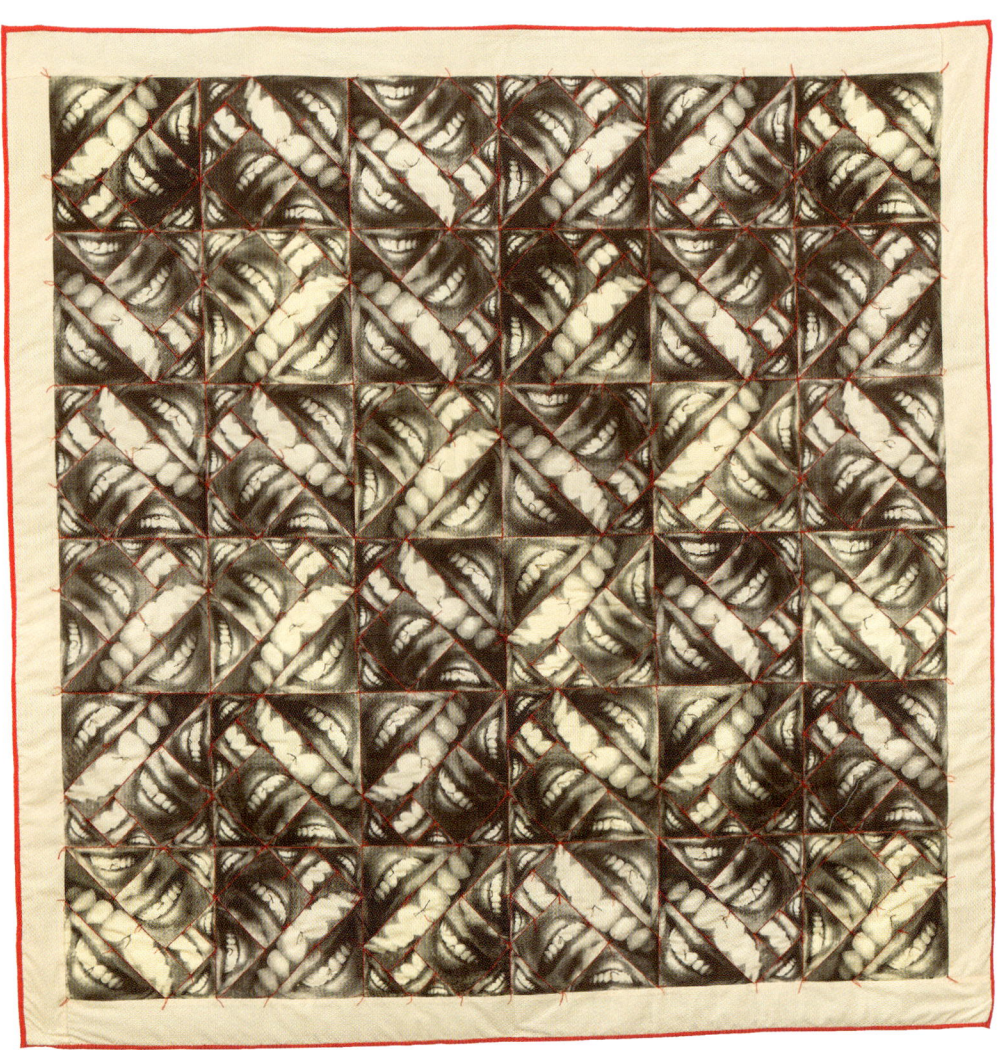

MARIE WOHADLO
Thompsonville, Michigan

Ballot Box
50″ x 50″

Cotton bed sheets, wool and poly "moving" blanket, linen tablecloth, thread, ink

Silkscreen, patchwork, hand tied, hand bound

Smiles, everyone, smiles!

We celebrate this exhibition with gratitude to our forebearers, pioneers who pushed the art form and opened up a new world, and we look toward the future, as the contemporary quilt community continues to carry the definition of quilting far beyond its traditional parameters and to promote quilt making as what it always has been—an art form.

THANK YOU
TO OUR 2017 QUILT NATIONAL SPONSORS

The quilts that are showcased in the 20th biennial of *Quilt National*, *Quilt National '17*, are presented here with gratitude to the sponsors, artists, organizers, board members, and attendees who have supported *Quilt National* over the years.

Friends of Fiber Arts

Nihon Vogue Co., Ltd/Japan Handicrafts Instructors' Association

Friends of Fiber Art International

Athens County Convention and Visitors Bureau

eQuilter.com

Ohio University Inn and Conference Center

The Crow Barn Art Retreats, Baltimore, Ohio, www.nancycrow.com

Hampton Inn

Nelsonville Quilt Company

Ohio Quilts

Ohio Arts Council

National Endowment for the Arts

Porter Financial Services

Quilt Surface Design Symposium

Studio Art Quilt Associates

Dedicated to Karen Nulf, former Quilt National *catalog graphic designer, board member, and friend.*

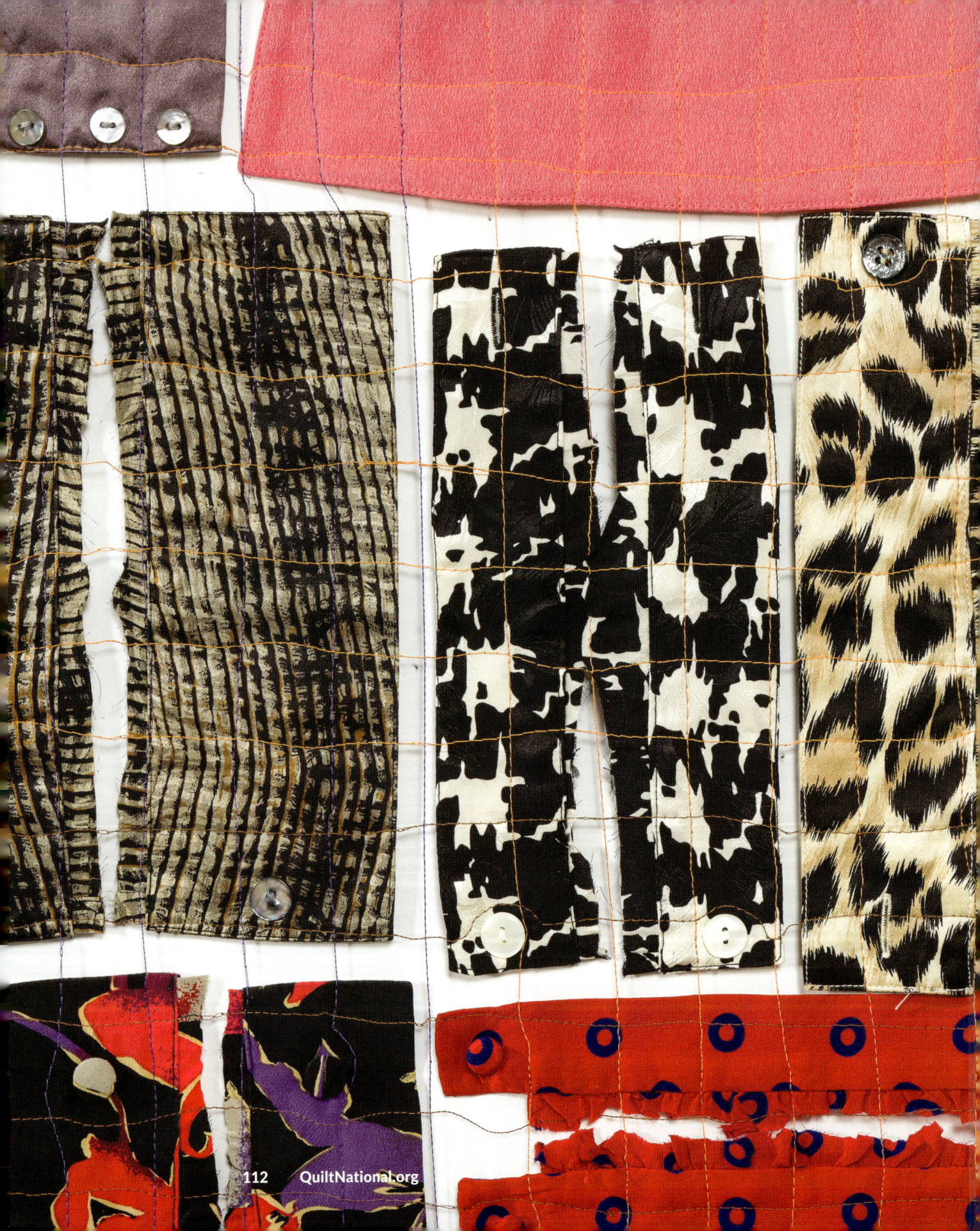

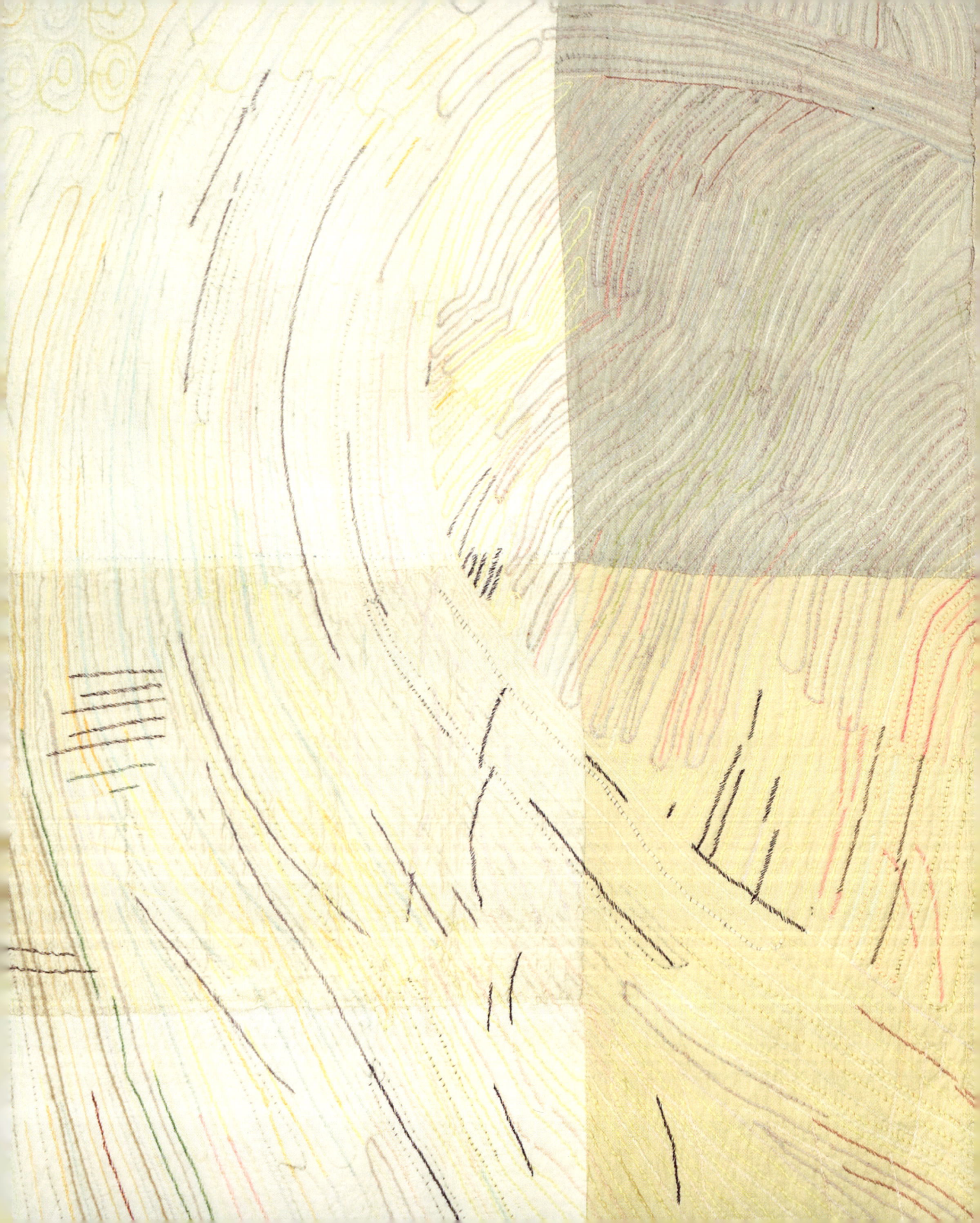